REVISE AQA GCSE (9–1) Spanish
REVISION WORKBOOK

Series Consultant: Harry Smith

Author: Vivien Halksworth

Also available to support your revision:

Revise GCSE Study Skills Guide   9781447967071

The **Revise GCSE Study Skills Guide** is full of tried-and-trusted hints and tips for how to learn more effectively. It gives you techniques to help you achieve your best – throughout your GCSE studies and beyond!

Revise GCSE Revision Planner   9781447967828

The **Revise GCSE Revision Planner** helps you to plan and organise your time, step-by-step, throughout your GCSE revision. Use this book and wall chart to mastermind your revision.

Difficulty scale

The scale next to each exam-style question tells you how difficult it is.

Some questions cover a range of difficulties.

The more of the scale that is shaded, the harder the question is.

 Some questions are Foundation level.

 Some questions are Higher level.

Some questions are applicable to both levels.

For the full range of Pearson revision titles across KS2, KS3, GCSE, Functional Skills, AS/A Level and BTEC visit:
www.pearsonschools.co.uk/revise

Contents

AUDIO

Audio files for the listening exercises in this book can be accessed by using the QR codes throughout the book, or going to www.pearsonschools.co.uk/mflrevisionaudio

Listen to the recording

A small bit of small print
AQA publishes Sample Assessment Material and the Specification on its website. This is the official content and this book should be used in conjunction with it. The questions in this Workbook have been written to help you practise every topic in the book. Remember: the real exam questions may not look like this.

1-to-1 page match with the Spanish Revision Guide ISBN 9781292131443

Physical descriptions

My new friend

1 Read the text that Jaime received from his Peruvian friend Santi.

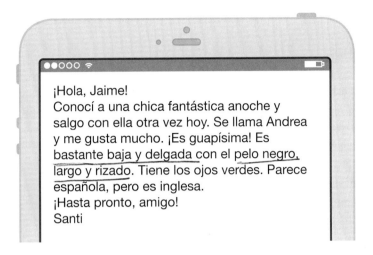

¡Hola, Jaime!
Conocí a una chica fantástica anoche y salgo con ella otra vez hoy. Se llama Andrea y me gusta mucho. ¡Es guapísima! Es bastante baja y delgada con el pelo negro, largo y rizado. Tiene los ojos verdes. Parece española, pero es inglesa.
¡Hasta pronto, amigo!
Santi

How does Santi describe Andrea?

A	tall and slim
B	small and slim
C	long, black, curly hair
D	short, black, curly hair
E	grey eyes
F	green eyes
G	really pretty
H	Spanish

Write the correct letters in the boxes.

Example

G   B   C   F

3
(3 marks)

Changing your appearance

2 Listen to these young people talking about themselves. Which aspect of their appearance would they like to change?

Answer in **English**.

> Always listen to the recording twice before making your decision and writing your answer.

Guided

Listen to the recording

Example: glasses

(a) ....   **(1 mark)**

(b) ....   **(1 mark)**

(c) ....   **(1 mark)**

(d) ....   **(1 mark)**

Character descriptions

A new TV series for children

1   Read this description of a new Spanish children's programme.

Una nueva serie de televisión

Martes, 5.15 de la tarde, empieza la nueva serie sobre las aventuras de cuatro chicos y su perro Tobi. Lucas, el chico mayor, es atrevido y valiente, pero siempre es muy responsable. La chica mayor se llama Dani. Es muy deportista y un poco loca a veces, pero no hay nadie más cariñoso que ella. Luego está Óscar, un chico muy serio e inteligente. Puede ser tímido, pero también discute mucho cuando sabe que tiene la razón. La más joven es Alicia, una chica amable y habladora, muy segura de sí misma a pesar de ser la menor.

What are the characters like? Answer the questions.

Example: Who is intelligent? Óscar

(a) Who is chatty? *Alicia* ....   ✓ **(1 mark)**

(b) Who is crazy? *Dani* ....   ✓ **(1 mark)**

(c) Who is daring? *Lucas* ....   ✓ **(1 mark)**

(d) Who is affectionate? *Dani* ....   ✓ **(1 mark)**

(e) Who is confident? *Alicia* ....   ✓ **(1 mark)**

(f) Who is shy? *Óscar* ....   ✓ **(1 mark)**

Translation

> I was = *era*
> they say that = *dicen que*

2   Translate the following sentences into **Spanish**.

(a) When I was young I was a bit shy and very serious.

> *Cuando era joven, era un poco tímida y muy seria*

(b) Now I am more sure of myself.

> *Ahora, soy más segura de mí mismo*

(c) I am an optimistic person.

> *Soy una persona optimista*

(d) My friends say that I am friendly.

> *Mis amigos dicen que soy amable / simpática*

(e) My parents think that I'm lazy.

> *Mis padres dicen que soy perezosa*
> *piensan*

10

(10 marks)

2

Describing family

Marta's family

1   Read this letter from your Spanish friend Marta about her family.

¡Hola, Gemma!

Antes de visitarnos en abril, deberías saber un poco de la familia con quien vas a vivir. En general, nos llevamos bien y hacemos muchas actividades juntos. Mis padres, Begoña y Pablo, están casados desde hace casi veinte años – es su aniversario pronto – y han vivido en este pueblo toda la vida. Mi hermano, Diego, es el hijo mayor y se parece mucho a mi padre. De vez en cuando tienen alguna disputa, pero nunca nada serio. Luego soy yo – dos años menor que Diego – y por último, Lucía, la pequeña, que solo tiene siete años. Nuestra abuela, Rosa, vive en la casa de al lado y comparte la casa con nuestra tía, Ana, que es soltera. Tenemos otros parientes en el pueblo, así que las celebraciones familiares pueden ser bastante grandes.

Estoy segura que te va a gustar nuestra familia y nuestros parientes. ¡Están locos, pero son muy amables!

Un abrazo:

Marta

Answer the questions in **English.**

> Be careful – the second question is worth two marks and the answer requires two names.

Example: Who is Marta's mother? Begoña

(a) Who looks like one of their parents? .Diego....................   **(1 mark)** ✓

(b) Who occasionally argue? ..Diego.y...Pablo.....   **(2 marks)** ✓✓

(c) Who is the youngest child? ..Lucia...................   **(1 mark)** ✓

(d) Who is Marta's grandmother? ..Rosa....................   **(1 mark)** ✓

(e) Who is the unmarried aunt? ....Ana...................   **(1 mark)** ✓

Laura's family

2   Listen to a podcast from your exchange partner Laura telling you about her family.

What does she say about her family?

Listen to the recording

A	Laura's parents divorced eleven years ago.
B	Laura is an only child.
C	Laura lives with her mother and stepfather.
D	Laura sometimes has to share a bedroom.
E	Laura's stepfather is called David.
F	Laura's stepbrother sometimes stays at the weekend.
G	Laura gets on well with her stepbrother.
H	Laura is older than her stepbrother.

Write the correct letters in the boxes.

☐   ☐   ☐   ☐   **(4 marks)**

Friends

The qualities of a friend

Listen to the recording

1 Listen to some Spanish friends talking about what is the **most** important quality in a friend.

How does each person describe the ideal friend?

Write the correct letter in each box.

> The speakers mention more than one quality, so having to pick out the **one** quality that is the **most** important makes this a more challenging task.

(a) Someone who …

A	shares your interests.
B	you can have fun with.
C	will always tell the truth.

☐ **(1 mark)**

(b) Someone who …

A	shares your sense of humour.
B	is prepared to listen to you.
C	can see your point of view.

☐ **(1 mark)**

(c) Someone who …

A	will keep your secrets.
B	you have a good time with.
C	you can talk to.

☐ **(1 mark)**

(d) Someone who …

A	is there for you.
B	helps with problems.
C	accepts you as you are.

☐ **(1 mark)**

Los amigos

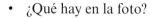

SPEAKING TRACK 4

2 Look at the photo and make any notes you wish. You will be asked the following three questions and then **two more questions** which you have not prepared.

- ¿Qué hay en la foto?
- ¿Qué tipo de amigo/a eres?
- ¿Cómo sería tu amigo o amiga ideal?

Listen to the recording

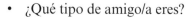

> Prepare your answers using the prompts. Then listen to the recording of the teacher's questions and answer in the pauses. There is a recording of one student's answers in the answer section to give you more ideas.

Relationships

A radio phone-in

Listen to the recording

1 Listen to a phone-in on Spanish radio giving advice about relationships. How is each person feeling about their relationship?

Write **P** for a **positive** opinion.
     N for a **negative** opinion.
     P+N for a **positive** and **negative** opinion.

(a) Sofía   ☐   **(1 mark)**

(b) Sebastián   ☐   **(1 mark)**

(c) Mariana   ☐   **(1 mark)**

(d) Alejandro   ☐   **(1 mark)**

(e) Gabriela   ☐   **(1 mark)**

Listen to the recording

Role play: una invitación

> Prepare your answers using the prompts. Then listen to the recording of the teacher's part and answer in the pauses. If you need more time, simply pause the recording. An example of a complete role play is recorded in the answer section.

2 Your Spanish exchange partner, Miranda, is busy on Saturday, but a friend of hers invites you both out for the day. The teacher will play the role of the friend and will speak first.

You must address the friend as *tú*. You will talk to the teacher using the five prompts below.

When you see this – **!** – you will have to respond to something you have not prepared.

When you see this – **?** – you will have to ask a question.

Estás hablando con la amiga de tu compañera española. La amiga os invita a salir.

1   La actividad de tu compañera

2   Tu aceptación y **una** razón

3   Tu preferencia: playa o montaña y **una** razón

4   **!**

5   **?** Relación con Miranda

> When accepting an invitation, you will need the conditional tense of *gustar*. To say 'Yes, I would really like that', you can say *'Sí, me gustaría mucho'* and then go on to give your reason.

Marriage and partnership

Las relaciones

1 Estás en casa de tu amigo español y ves estos comentarios en un sitio web sobre las relaciones.

Verónica	Daniel y yo llevamos saliendo casi dos años y anoche me dio una gran sorpresa. Vino a casa y me pidió que me casara con él. ¡Qué emoción! Claro que dije que sí, y me dio un hermoso anillo de diamantes
Alejandro	Anoche mi hermano Santi me llamó para hablar de los problemas que tiene con su esposa. Parece que las cosas han estado muy mal entre ellos desde hace más de un año y ha decidido dejar la casa que comparten para alquilar un piso él solo.
Alba	A mí lo que más me atrae es la independencia. Quizás es por tener padres bastante estrictos pero mi sueño es vivir sola, tener mis propias reglas y hacer lo que me dé la gana. No tengo ninguna intención de casarme.
Jorge	Mis abuelos están casados desde hace sesenta años y este fin de semana hemos organizado una fiesta para celebrarlo. No saben que hemos reservado una mesa grande en un restaurante y que nos reuniremos casi treinta personas.

¿De qué hablan los jóvenes?

A	el amor
B	el compromiso
C	el matrimonio
D	el aniversario
E	la boda
F	la separación
G	el divorcio
H	estar soltero

Escribe la letra correcta en cada casilla.

(a) Verónica   B ✓   **(1 mark)**   (c) Alba   H ✓   **(1 mark)**

(b) Alejandro   F ✓   **(1 mark)**   (d) Jorge   D ✓   **(1 mark)**

Relationships

2 Listen to your Spanish friends Pablo and Cristina talking about relationships.

What is their opinion of these aspects?

Write **P** for a **positive** opinion.
    N for a **negative** opinion.
    P+N for a **positive** and **negative** opinion.

(a) **Pablo**

   marriage ☐   weddings ☐   **(2 marks)**

(b) **Cristina**

   divorce ☐   being single ☐   **(2 marks)**

When I was younger

Entrevista con un escritor

1   Read an online interview with the author Carlos Vargas Márquez, who is describing his childhood.

Carlos, ¿cómo eras de niño?

De niño, pasaba bastante tiempo solo porque era hijo único, pero tenía una gran imaginación. Si jugaba en mi dormitorio, imaginaba que la cama era una isla desierta en medio del mar. Cuando jugaba al aire libre, creía que el jardín era un bosque tropical con animales salvajes. No tenía mucho éxito como estudiante y no sacaba buenas notas, pero siempre leía mucho y escribía pequeñas historias.

Carlos Vargas Márquez

Answer the questions in **English.**

(a) Why did Carlos spend a lot of time alone? *He was an only child*

.... **(1 mark)**

(b) In his imagination when he was playing, what did these things become?

(i)   his bed *A deserted island in the middle of the sea*

.... **(1 mark)**

(ii)   the garden *A tropical forest with wild animals*

.... **(1 mark)**

(c) What indicates that he was not a good student? *He didn't get good*

grades .... **(1 mark)**

(d) What were the early signs that he would become an author? *He was always*

reading a lot and was writing short stories. .... **(2 marks)**

> The number of marks is a clue to the amount of information expected in the answer. Make sure that you give **two** signs in (d).

Interview with a writer

2   Listen to the second part of the interview online. Which three statements are true?

A	He lived all his life in the country.
B	He played outdoors a lot.
C	He used to camp in the garden.
D	His cousins bought him a bike.
E	He played happily with his cousins.
F	He looks back fondly on his childhood.

Write the correct letters in the boxes.

☐   ☐   ☐   **(3 marks)**

Social media

Opinions on social media

1 Read the following comments in an online forum.

A	Acabo de cerrar mi cuenta porque me molestaba leer la misma basura todo el tiempo. No quería ver más vídeos de mascotas haciendo cosas divertidas ni las fotos de las vacaciones de todo el mundo. Francamente, me aburría. **Laura**
B	Yo creo que a veces la gente es demasiado honesta con lo que dice en esas páginas. Imagina que vas a una entrevista y, después, el empresario mira tu página en una red social. ¿Hay información allí que no quieres que vea? Pues cuidado. **Jaime**
C	Soy profesora y me ha sorprendido que estas redes también puedan usarse en la enseñanza. Resulta que una de mis clases ha creado una página y los estudiantes pueden escribir preguntas allí que sus compañeros contestan. ¡Qué maravilla! **Mariana**
D	Para mí, estas páginas son muy divertidas pero una distracción terrible. Cuando estoy haciendo mis deberes en el ordenador, siempre estoy contestando los mensajes que aparecen en la pantalla en lugar de concentrarme en escribir mi ensayo. **Teo**

Write the correct letter in each box.

Example: Who doesn't want to see any more funny pet videos?   A

(a) Who warns people to beware of what they write?   ☐ **(1 mark)**

(b) Who has just closed a social media account?   ☐ **(1 mark)**

(c) Who finds that social networks stop you doing other things?   ☐ **(1 mark)**

(d) Who is impressed by the way some young people use social networks?   ☐ **(1 mark)**

(e) Who worries that a company boss might look at an applicant's page?   ☐ **(1 mark)**

(f) Who would recommend social networks as a useful educational tool?   ☐ **(1 mark)**

Las redes sociales

2 Decides contribuir a un blog sobre el uso de las redes sociales.

Escribe tus ideas para el blog.

Menciona:

- qué te gusta de las redes sociales
- qué te preocupa de las redes sociales
- cómo has usado una red social recientemente
- cómo vas a usar las redes sociales este fin de semana y por qué.

En otra hoja de papel, escribe aproximadamente **90** palabras en **español**.
Responde a todos los aspectos de la pregunta.   **(16 marks)**

Technology

My friends and technology

1 Read these text messages from your Spanish friends.

A Alicia

> Acabo de comprar un nuevo portátil, pero el teclado es muy difícil de usar.

C Carla

> Mi nuevo videojuego es muy difícil, pero he bajado una aplicación útil.

B Begoña

> Mi ordenador está roto, así que mi padre me ha dado su tableta antigua.

D Daniela

> He olvidado mi contraseña y no puedo acceder a mi página web.

Write the correct letter in each box.

Example: Who has been given a new tablet? ☐ B

(a) Who has downloaded a good app? ☐ **(1 mark)**

(b) Who complains about the keyboard? ☐ **(1 mark)**

(c) Who has forgotten her password? ☐ **(1 mark)**

(d) Who has found that her computer is broken? ☐ **(1 mark)**

(e) Who is writing about a laptop? ☐ **(1 mark)**

Role play: technology

2 You are discussing technology with your Spanish friend. The teacher will play the role of your friend and will speak first.

You must address the friend as *tú*. You will talk to the teacher using the five prompts below.

Listen to the recording

> Prepare your answers using the prompts. Then listen to the recording of the teacher's part and answer in the pauses. If you need more time, simply pause the recording. An example of a complete role play is recorded in the answer section.

Estás hablando de tecnología con tu amigo español / tu amiga española.

1 Tu uso de la tecnología (**un** detalle)

2 Tu opinión de las tabletas (**un** detalle)

3 !

4 El coste de la tecnología (**un** detalle)

5 ? Página web favorita

> For the unprepared point, it is of course essential to listen carefully to the question you are being asked. However, it is fine to ask your teacher to repeat the question, twice at the most. To do so, you can say: ¿*Puedes repetirlo?* (Can you repeat it?) or *Más despacio, por favor* (More slowly, please).

The internet

Internet for all ages

1 Read Jorge's account of how his family uses the internet.

> En mi casa somos muy aficionados a Internet y sus muchos usos. Yo soy Jorge y soy estudiante en la universidad. Uso Internet para buscar información y hacer investigaciones. También suelo bajar canciones, usar las redes sociales y subir fotos. Mi padre siempre está mandando y recibiendo correos electrónicos relacionados con su trabajo, lo que le molesta mucho a mi madre. Incluso mi hermana pequeña, Cristina, usa Internet para aprender con juegos educativos o ver vídeos para niños. Mi madre estudia inglés y le gusta hacer ejercicios interactivos para practicar.

(a) Which **two** statements are true?
Write the correct letters in the boxes.

A	Jorge emails essays to his university tutors.
B	Jorge downloads music.
C	Jorge's father often shops online.
D	Jorge's mother watches exercise and fitness videos.
E	Jorge's mother does activities to practise English.

☐ ☐ **(2 marks)**

(b) In what **two** ways does Cristina use the internet?
Answer in **English**.

.... **(2 marks)**

Using the internet

Listen to the recording

2 Listen to some Spanish friends who are discussing their use of the internet.
How do they use it?

A	reading emails
B	sending messages
C	looking for work
D	playing games

E	social networking
F	online shopping
G	booking flights
H	surfing the web

Write the correct letter in each box.

(a) Ana ☐ **(1 mark)** (c) David ☐ **(1 mark)**

(b) Elena ☐ **(1 mark)** (d) Pedro ☐ **(1 mark)**

Translation

⟩ **Guided**

3 Translate this passage into **English**. Write your answer on a separate piece of paper.

> Yo no puedo imaginar la vida sin Internet porque en mi casa solemos usarlo todos los días. Si olvidas el nombre de una película o quieres saber cuándo nació cierto autor, Internet tiene todas las repuestas. Además, ha cambiado la manera en que hacemos nuestras compras.

I can't imagine life without the internet .... **(9 marks)**

Pros and cons of technology

Concerns about technology

1 Listen to some Spanish friends discussing their concerns about technology.

Write the correct letter in each box.

Example: Pedro has just had a lesson in …

A	Maths.
B	IT.
C	Food technology.

B

(a) Luisa knows a girl who …

A	had her identity stolen.
B	sent money to a swindler.
C	was upset by online bullying.

☐ **(1 mark)**

(b) Rafael's father …

A	had his bank account hacked from abroad.
B	went into the bank when he suspected fraud.
C	has set up security controls on his account.

☐ **(1 mark)**

(c) Sandra …

A	showed her parents how to set controls.
B	worries about what sites young children might see.
C	met someone she got to know online.

☐ **(1 mark)**

(d) Pedro …

A	says that technology is making us lazy.
B	plays a lot of tennis with his friends.
C	forgot a tennis match because he was online.

☐ **(1 mark)**

Lo bueno y lo malo de Internet

> Prepare your answers using the prompts. Then listen to the recording of the teacher's questions and answer in the pauses. There is a recording of one student's answers in the answer section to give you more ideas.

2 Look at the photo and make any notes you wish. You will be asked the following three questions and then **two more questions** which you have not prepared.

- ¿Qué hay en la foto?
- ¿Qué problemas hay con Internet?
- ¿Cuáles son los aspectos buenos de Internet?

Hobbies

Favourite hobbies

1 Read these contributions to a forum about birthday presents.

A	Lo ideal para mí sería recibir unas botas de patinaje de mi marca favorita. No me interesan los perfumes ni el maquillaje. **Adela**
B	Lo que yo quiero es aprender a tocar la batería: cinco clases gratuitas serían perfectas. Nada de accesorios deportivos. **Benjamín**
C	El año pasado mi tía me regaló un vídeo de dibujos animados. ¡Qué regalo tan tonto! Este año me gustaría recibir dos entradas para el torneo de baloncesto. **Celia**
D	Lo peor es cuando te regalan calcetines o camisetas. Me aburre un montón. El mejor regalo: un nuevo móvil – el último modelo. **Daniel**

Write the correct letter in each box.

Example: Who does not like cartoons?   ☐ C

(a) Who would like sporting equipment?   ☐   **(1 mark)**

(b) Who does **not** want to be given clothes?   ☐   **(1 mark)**

(c) Who wants to watch a live match?   ☐   **(1 mark)**

(d) Who wants music tuition?   ☐   **(1 mark)**

(e) Who would prefer **not** to receive cosmetics?   ☐   **(1 mark)**

Mis pasatiempos

2 Quieres ir a España para trabajar en un club de niños en un camping.

Escribe un correo electrónico al jefe describiendo tus pasatiempos para demostrar que eres la persona adecuada para el trabajo. Menciona:

- los deportes que haces
- los otros pasatiempos que tienes
- cuándo haces estas actividades
- por qué te gustan estas actividades.

Escribe aproximadamente **40** palabras en **español**.

....

....

....

....

....

....

....

....

> Remember: when talking about playing an instrument, use the verb *tocar* for 'to play'. However, for 'playing' a game or sport you use *jugar*. When talking about 'doing' an activity, such as riding or skating, you use *hacer*.

(16 marks)

Music

A music blog

1 Read these comments in a blog about music.

> **Blog de música. Escribe tu opinión o tus experiencias.**
>
> **A** Mi padre nunca tuvo la oportunidad de aprender un instrumento cuando era joven, así que mañana empieza clases de guitarra. Yo uso la música para ayudarme a hacer los trabajos que no me gustan. No me importa lavar el coche o arreglar mi dormitorio si puedo escuchar música. **David**
>
> **B** Mi grupo favorito dio un concierto anoche, pero fue una pena que solo cantaran las canciones de su nuevo álbum. Fue un poco decepcionante. Canto con un coro una vez a la semana y es muy relajante. Sin embargo, ahora estoy nervioso porque damos un concierto este viernes. **Eduardo**
>
> **C** A veces no quería ir a las clases de piano cuando era pequeño, pero ahora, tocar el piano es lo que más me gusta en la vida. Practiqué con la banda ayer y a todos les gustan las canciones que he escrito. ¡Genial! **Fernando**
>
> **D** Mis padres no entienden por qué pongo música cuando estoy haciendo los deberes, pero no hay duda de que ayuda a mejorar la concentración. **Juan**

Write the correct letter in each box.

Example: Who says that his dad is learning to play an instrument?   A

(a) Who is glad he carried on with his music lessons?   ☐   **(1 mark)**

(b) Who says that the idea of performing is a bit nerve-racking?   ☐   **(1 mark)**

(c) Who feels that he studies better with music on?   ☐   **(1 mark)**

(d) Who felt that it was a shame the band didn't play their old hits?   ☐   **(1 mark)**

(e) Who is relieved that the group likes his songs?   ☐   **(1 mark)**

(f) Who thinks that music is useful to take your mind off boring jobs?   ☐   **(1 mark)**

Juan Zelada, musician

2 You listen to a radio programme describing an interview with Juan Zelada.

Listen to the recording and answer the questions below in English.

(a) Why is Juan here? ....   **(1 mark)**

Listen to the recording

(b) What does he say about
   (i)   breakfast? ....   **(1 mark)**
   (ii) his music? ....   **(1 mark)**

(c) What does he usually do
   (i)   in the mornings? ....   **(1 mark)**
   (ii) in the evenings? ....   **(1 mark)**

(d) Why does he not sleep? ....   **(1 mark)**

(e) What does he do once every week? ....   **(1 mark)**

(f) Why does he do this? ....   **(1 mark)**

Music events

Concerts

1 Read these opinions on a forum from people who went to a recent concert.

A	Una gran noche para mis amigos y yo. El guitarrista de la banda estuvo fenomenal. Lástima que no tocaran más tiempo. **Raúl**
B	¡Qué bien lo pasamos! Gracias a la banda por tocar sus viejas canciones, además de las más recientes. **Lidia**
C	Si os digo la verdad, no lo pasé muy bien. Fui con una amiga que quería ver al grupo, pero ese tipo de música no es de mi gusto. **Iván**
D	Fui al concierto sin conocer su música y ahora soy su mayor fan. Compré una camiseta al final del concierto y hoy compré el CD. **Celia**

Which person makes each statement? You can use each letter more than once.

Write the correct letter in each box.

Example: Who thinks the guitarist was fantastic? ☐ A

(a) Who only went to keep a friend company? ☐ **(1 mark)**

(b) Who didn't know the band beforehand? ☐ **(1 mark)**

(c) Who felt the band should have played longer? ☐ **(1 mark)**

(d) Who was pleased with the range of songs played? ☐ **(1 mark)**

(e) Who has bought some band merchandise? ☐ **(1 mark)**

(f) Who didn't enjoy the type of music? ☐ **(1 mark)**

Taking part

2 Listen to your Valencian friend Andrés talking about a musical event he is involved in. What does he mention?

Listen to the recording

A	the cost of the tickets
B	where the concert will be
C	the type of music they will play
D	what the concert is in aid of
E	the starting time
F	the date of the concert
G	how many people are in the orchestra
H	the instrument he plays

Write the correct letters in the boxes.

Example

H ☐ ☐ ☐ **(3 marks)**

> Remember that in this type of exercise you won't hear words like *fecha* (date) or *donde* (where), the English equivalent of which you see in the questions. Instead, you will hear a day or month, giving a date, and a location or venue, indicating where the concert is.

Sport

Beach volleyball

1 Read this advert for a forthcoming sporting event. Write the correct letter in each box.

Gran Fiesta Voleibol Playa

¿No sabes qué hacer estas vacaciones?

¿Quieres hacer ejercicio pero también buscas mucha diversión?

¡Pues esta fiesta es para ti!

Para jóvenes de entre trece y diecisiete años, este curso es ideal no solo para mejorar tus habilidades deportivas, especialmente las de equipo. También es una gran oportunidad para conocer nuevos amigos.

Si te interesa …

Ven el lunes día 3 a la cala de Mogán – zona verde.

Trae bañador, ropa deportiva y comida

(todos los refrescos están incluidos).

Precio: 15 euros el día.

Imprescindible autorización de padres o tutores.

Example: This activity is for people who want to have …

A	fun.
B	a holiday.
C	a summer job.

(a) The festival is for …

A	all ages.
B	parents.
C	teenagers.

☐

(b) One skill you might improve is …

A	speaking another language.
B	being a team player.
C	communication.

☐

(c) You need to bring …

A	a ball.
B	drinks.
C	appropriate clothing.

☐

(d) Participation will not be possible without …

A	parental consent.
B	pre-booking.
C	some form of identification.

☐

(4 marks)

Sport

2 You overhear four young people talking about sport. Which sports do they mention? Write the correct letters in the boxes.

> Guided

Listen to the recording

A	football
B	cycling
C	swimming
D	athletics
E	basketball
F	skiing
G	skating
H	horse riding

For this type of question, use the five-minute reading time at the start of the exam to read the sports and think about what they are in Spanish. That way you will be better prepared to listen out for the ones that come up.

A ☐ ☐ ☐

(4 marks)

Sporting events

The big match

1 Read this extract from *Sara y las goleadoras* by Laura Gallego.

> Mientras sus rivales celebraban el gol (con poco entusiasmo, como si lo que acababan de hacer no fuera nada del otro mundo), Sara y sus amigas regresaron a sus posiciones con la cabeza baja, sin atreverse a mirar a las gradas,* desde donde las observaban los chicos.
>
> Sara miró el reloj: no llevaban ni diez minutos de partido y ya perdían por un gol. Pero lo peor no era eso; después de todo, un gol se podía remontar. No, lo peor de todo había sido aquella sensación de impotencia ante un equipo que era mucho mejor que el suyo.
>
> Angustiada, Sara volvió la vista hacia su entrenador, pero él le indicó con gestos que se calmara. Aún quedaba mucho partido por delante.

Answer the following questions in **English.**

*gradas = terraces

(a) What had the rival team done at the start of the extract?

.... **(1 mark)**

(b) How does the text describe the body language of Sara and the girls?

.... **(1 mark)**

(c) Why didn't the girls want to look at the terraces?

.... **(1 mark)**

(d) What was the score ten minutes into the match?

.... **(1 mark)**

(e) What did Sara conclude about the other team?

.... **(1 mark)**

(f) What was their trainer trying to communicate?

.... **(1 mark)**

Local sports events

2 Listen to your Spanish friend talking about sporting events near his home. What does he say? Write the correct letter in each box.

Listen to the recording

Example: During the cycle race …

A	the city gets too crowded.
B	**there's a festival atmosphere.**
C	there are television crews all over.

B

(a) The local football club …

A	provides employment for many.
B	is having building work done.
C	charges a fortune for merchandise.

☐ **(1 mark)**

(b) The recent athletics championship …

A	was postponed due to bad weather.
B	took place last month.
C	was sold out.

☐ **(1 mark)**

(c) The swimming event …

A	caused huge traffic problems.
B	provided a great new facility.
C	was poorly attended.

☐ **(1 mark)**

Films

Listen to the recording

Film descriptions

1　What type of film is showing in screens 1–4? Write the correct letter in each box.

A	a science-fiction film
B	a romantic film
C	a comedy
D	an adventure film
E	a sporting success story
F	a horror film
G	a historical drama
H	a crime thriller

Example: Screen 1　☐ D

(a)　Screen 2　☐　　　　　　　　　　　　　　　　　　　　　　　**(1 mark)**

(b)　Screen 3　☐　　　　　　　　　　　　　　　　　　　　　　　**(1 mark)**

(c)　Screen 4　☐　　　　　　　　　　　　　　　　　　　　　　　**(1 mark)**

Sara y las goleadoras by Laura Gallego

2　Read the extract from the text. The girls are members of a football team arranging to go out.

> Guided

> –Oye, yo voy a ir este sábado al cine con unas amigas, ¿por qué no os venís Vicky y tú, y las que queráis? –dijo Lidia.
>
> –Vicky no querrá, tiene que estudiar; y a Eva seguro que sus padres no la dejan. –Sara contestó. – Pero lo diré a las demás; seguro que alguna se apunta. ¡Qué buena idea!
>
> Ángela y Alicia tenían ganas de ir, e Isa y Julia también estuvieron de acuerdo, de modo que terminaron siendo un grupo muy numeroso.
>
> Lo pasaron bien en el cine, y después fueron a merendar, y se rieron mucho comentando los mejores momentos de la película (Isa hizo una magistral imitación, muy dramática, de la actriz protagonista).

Answer the questions in **English**.

Example: What does Lidia invite Sara and her friends to do and when?
Go to the cinema on Saturday

(a)　Why won't Vicky go? ....　**(1 mark)**

(b)　Why does Sara think Eva won't go? ....　**(1 mark)**

(c)　How do we know they had fun? Give **one** reason. ....　**(1 mark)**

(d)　What did they discuss afterwards? ....　**(1 mark)**

(e)　How did Isa entertain them? ....　**(1 mark)**

TV

TV programmes

1 Read José's list of favourite TV programmes. What is on his list?

Write the correct letters in the boxes.

las noticias

los dibujos animados

las telenovelas

los documentales

las películas de terror

A	news
B	sports programmes
C	cartoons
D	quiz shows
E	documentaries
F	horror films
G	music concerts
H	soaps
I	adverts

Example: F ☐ ☐ ☐ ☐

(4 marks)

Marisa's viewing habits

2 Listen to Marisa, your Spanish friend, talking about television programmes. Answer the questions in **English**.

Example: What does Marisa love watching? adventure programmes

Listen to the recording

(a) What does she like watching best? .... **(1 mark)**

(b) What can't she stand? .... **(1 mark)**

(c) What does she never watch? .... **(1 mark)**

(d) What does she think of soaps? .... **(1 mark)**

La televisión

3 Tu amiga Marta te pregunta sobre lo que ves en la televisión.

Escribe una respuesta.
Menciona:

> Try to avoid using lots of English titles when you are talking or writing about television. That won't show off your Spanish. Instead, mention types of programmes, as José does in exercise 1: this way you will ensure that you use good Spanish vocabulary.

- cuándo te gusta ver la televisión
- los programas que no te gustan
- los programas que vas a ver esta noche
- tus programas favoritos cuando eras pequeño/a.

Escribe aproximadamente **90** palabras en **español**.

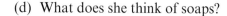

....

....

....

....

....

....

.... **(16 marks)**

Food and drink

Eating out

1 Listen to these young Spanish people talking about what they are going to eat or drink.

Complete the sentences. Answer in **English**.

(a) Magda is having a ham .... **(1 mark)**

(b) Pablo is having a .... yoghurt. **(1 mark)**

(c) María is having a cheese .... **(1 mark)**

(d) Santi is having .... juice. **(1 mark)**

Listen to the recording

A birthday meal

2 Read this email from your Spanish friend Jorge about his birthday meal.

> ✉
>
> Anoche comimos en el mejor restaurante de mi pueblo para celebrar mi cumpleaños. A mí me gustaron más el atún y las sardinas. Mi padre prefirió las brochetas de pollo y el filete de cerdo. A mi hermano le gustó más el entrante de judías y guisantes. A mi hermana le gustó más el postre de melocotón y fresas.

¿Qué aspecto de la cena le gustó más a cada miembro de la familia?

A	carne
B	ensalada
C	fruta
D	legumbres
E	pescado
F	vino

Escribe la letra correcta en cada casilla.

(a) Jorge ☐ **(1 mark)**　　(c) su hermano ☐ **(1 mark)**

(b) su padre ☐ **(1 mark)**　　(d) su hermana ☐ **(1 mark)**

Translation

3 Translate this passage into **English.**

> Me gusta mucho ir de tapas porque puedes probar una variedad de platos. En Galicia, donde vivo, la especialidad es el pescado y anoche tomé mariscos en una salsa muy sabrosa. Este fin de semana vamos a salir a cenar con mis abuelos y comeré bistec.

Guided

I really like going ....

....

....

....

.... **(9 marks)**

Eating in a café

In a café

1 Some friends are ordering in a café in Murcia. What do they order?

Listen to the recording

A	a vanilla ice cream
B	a coffee with milk
C	a portion of omelette
D	a strawberry ice cream
E	a sandwich
F	sparkling water
G	an orange juice
H	a hot dog

Write the correct letter in each box.

Example: Juan Martín   F

(a) Isabel   ☐   **(1 mark)**

(b) Sofía   ☐   **(1 mark)**

(c) Rubén   ☐   **(1 mark)**

Role play: ordering in a café

> Prepare your answers using the prompts. Then listen to the recording of the teacher's part and answer in the pauses. If you need more time, simply pause the recording. An example of a complete role play is recorded in the answer section.

Listen to the recording

2 You are with a Spanish friend in a café in Valencia and are ordering drinks and a snack. The teacher will play the part of your friend and will speak first.

You must address your friend as *tú*. You will talk to the teacher using the five prompts below.

Estás con tu amigo/a en una cafetería y pides algo para beber y comer.

1 Bebida – tipo   4 Opinión sobre la comida española

2 Algo para comer   5 ? Precio

3 !

> You need to learn how to ask what something costs: ask either *¿Cuánto es?* or *¿Cuánto cuesta?*

Friends in a café

3 Mandas esta foto de tu hermana y sus amigos a tu amigo español.

Describe la foto. Escribe **cuatro** frases en **español**.

....

....

....

....

....   **(12 marks)**

Eating in a restaurant

Eating out

1   You are eating out with friends in Madrid and they need your advice about the menu.

Menú del día	12 €	Incluido: Pan, vino y café
Entrantes	**Platos principales**	**Postres**
Espaguetis	Pollo	Melocotón
Ensalada	Bistec	Tarta de manzana
Sopa de tomate	Tortilla de patatas	Helado

What do you recommend to each friend? Write your answers in **English**.

Example: It's hot so I want a very cold dessert. *ice cream*

(a) I want a cold starter.   ....   **(1 mark)**

(b) I'd like a vegetarian main course.   ....   **(1 mark)**

(c) I really like pasta.   ....   **(1 mark)**

(d) I just want fruit for dessert.   ....   **(1 mark)**

(e) I only eat white meat.   ....   **(1 mark)**

In a restaurant

Listen to the recording

2   You hear a man ordering for himself and his family in a restaurant. What does he ask the waitress about?

A	the fish dish
B	what is included in the menu
C	the price of the menu of the day
D	what ingredients are in a dish
E	smaller portions for children
F	a dessert that is dairy-free
G	a recommendation for a wine
H	the types of coffee available

Write the correct letters in the boxes.

Example: C ☐   ☐   ☐   ☐   **(3 marks)**

Meals at home

Cooking and eating

Listen to the
recording

1   Listen to these people talking about meals at home.

What does each one say? Answer in **English**.

(a)   Carla   ....   **(1 mark)**

(b)   David   ....   **(1 mark)**

(c)   Nuria   ....   **(1 mark)**

(d)   Ricardo ....   **(1 mark)**

Listen to the
recording

2

Look at the photo and make any notes you wish. You will be asked the following three questions and then **two more questions** which you have not prepared.

- ¿Qué hay en la foto?
- ¿Cuál es una comida típica en tu casa?
- ¿Qué tomaste para comer el fin de semana pasado?

> Prepare your answers using the prompts. Then listen to the recording of the teacher's questions and answer in the pauses. There is a recording of one student's answers in the answer section to give you more ideas.

Shopping for food

A shopping list

1 Read this note from your Spanish exchange partner's mother.

Hola chicos

¿Podéis ir a las tiendas para comprarme estas cosas?
He dejado dinero en la mesa de la cocina.

Mercado

medio kilo de plátanos

un kilo de cebollas

un pepino

medio kilo de zanahorias

Supermercado

una docena de huevos grandes

cien gramos de jamón

una caja de galletas (podéis escoger el tipo)

una lata de atún

Answer the following questions in **English.**

(a) Where has she left the money for the shopping? .... **(1 mark)**

(b) How many carrots should they get? .... **(1 mark)**

(c) Where should they get the onions? .... **(1 mark)**

(d) What fruit do they need to buy? .... **(1 mark)**

(e) What have they got to choose? .... **(1 mark)**

(f) How much ham should they get? .... **(1 mark)**

(g) What is the last item on the supermarket list? .... **(1 mark)**

Role play: going shopping

Prepare your answers using the prompts. Then listen to the recording of the teacher's part and answer in the pauses. If you need more time, simply pause the recording. An example of a complete role play is recorded in the answer section.

Listen to the recording

2 You are shopping for food in Tarragona. The teacher will play the part of the shop assistant and will speak first.

You must address the shop assistant as *usted.* You will talk to the teacher using the five prompts below.

Estás comprando comida en una tienda en Tarragona. Hablas con el dependiente / la dependienta.

1 Fruta – tipo

2 **!**

3 Algo para beber

4 Algo para poner en un bocadillo – cantidad

5 **?** Precio

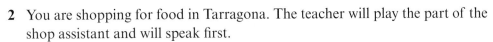

Remember that the prompts will never provide you with the vocabulary you need, so when you are asked to order fruit, you must think of a type, such as *plátanos, manzanas* or *naranjas.*

23

Opinions about food

European cuisine

1 Read this article about food in Europe.

He pasado quince años viajando por Europa y escribiendo artículos para los periódicos sobre los platos que he probado. Mi conclusión es que la comida europea se destaca por la variedad enorme, no de los ingredientes usados, sino de los métodos de cocinar. Los cocineros de la gran mayoría de los países se esfuerzan mucho por utilizar los productos regionales en la temporada apropiada. Por eso, en las zonas costeras se ven muchos mariscos y donde hay campos verdes encontrarás queso de cabra y carne de vaca.

Sin embargo, hay características nacionales notables que diferencian a los países. En Francia aprecian las salsas ricas en mantequilla mientras que en Italia disfrutan más de los productos de alta calidad preparados simplemente. En Gran Bretaña son famosas las tartas y los pasteles, pero en España prefieren tomar algo mucho más ligero para el postre, como una manzana o un yogur.

Write the correct letter in each box.

Example: The author …

A	is writing a book about Europe.
B	cooks European food.
C	is a journalist.

C

(a) In Europe there is a lot of variety in …

A	how they prepare the dishes.
B	the way they grow the ingredients.
C	the equipment used in the kitchen.

☐

(b) The chefs have in common that they …

A	buy from local producers.
B	experiment with exotic ingredients.
C	grow a lot of their own food.

☐

(c) What might you find in a green area?

A	fruit and vegetables
B	cereal crops
C	cattle farming

☐

(d) Which country is said to prefer plainer food?

A	France
B	Italy
C	Great Britain

☐

(e) Where are you more likely to get a heavier dessert?

A	France
B	Italy
C	Great Britain

☐

(5 marks)

> The translation task will always test more than one tense, so before you start read the text through and look out for tenses other than the present. Here, there are references to both the past and the future as well as the present.

Translation

2 Traduce el texto siguiente al **español**. Escribe la traducción en una hoja de papel.

I like Spanish food a lot and the restaurant near the church makes really good food. The fish is very tasty and I loved the spicy sausage that I had last week. The food is always appetizing and, in my opinion, it is fairly healthy. We are going to eat there on Friday and I will try the seafood.

(12 marks)

Celebrations

Special days

1 Read these accounts of celebrations on a forum.

A	La Nochevieja siempre es muy divertida en mi casa y el año pasado mis padres dieron una fiesta. A medianoche, claro, celebramos con las doce uvas, intentando comer una uva cada vez que sonó* la campana.** **Andrés**
B	En mi casa mantenemos la vieja costumbre de dar regalos de navidad el Día de Reyes. Podemos abrir un solo regalo el día de Navidad y tenemos que esperar hasta el seis de enero para abrir los demás. **Beatriz**
C	De niño, me gustaba la Nochebuena porque había una cena especial y siempre empezábamos con mariscos. Era una tarde emocionante porque toda la familia se reunía para celebrar la ocasión. **Carlos**
D	En Inglaterra, las fiestas navideñas son un poco diferentes. Siempre abren los regalos la mañana del 25 y comen la comida principal sobre la una o las dos. ¡Muchas personas se duermen después! **Daniela**

Who talks about each of the following? Write the correct letter in each box.

*sonar = to chime
**la campana = bell

Example: New Year's Eve A

(a) Christmas Eve   ☐   **(1 mark)**

(b) 6 January   ☐   **(1 mark)**

(c) eating fruit   ☐   **(1 mark)**

(d) eating seafood   ☐   **(1 mark)**

(e) Christmas lunch   ☐   **(1 mark)**

(f) keeping up old traditions ☐   **(1 mark)**

Special events

2 Listen to a trailer about today's soap opera episodes.
   What celebrations are taking place?

A	birth of baby
B	New Year
C	anniversary
D	wedding
E	retirement
F	Christmas
G	birthday

Always listen to the whole recording and try not to base your answer on just hearing one word. For example, if you hear *matrimonio* you will need to keep listening so that you can decide whether it is a wedding or a wedding anniversary.

Listen to the recording

Write the correct letter in each box.

Example: 'Los Vecinos'   F

(a) 'Esmeralda'   ☐   **(1 mark)**

(b) 'La Calle Pozo'   ☐   **(1 mark)**

(c) 'Hotel Miramar'   ☐   **(1 mark)**

Customs

Spanish customs

1 Listen to your Spanish friends explaining some of their customs. What does each one say?

Write the correct answer in each box.

(a) Having tapas is …

A	becoming popular outside Spain.
B	a snack rather than a full meal.
C	going out of fashion in Spain.

☐

(1 mark)

(b) The Spanish stroll …

A	is an after-lunch activity.
B	takes place in the main street.
C	doesn't happen on Sundays.

☐

(1 mark)

(c) The bull fight …

A	is a very old custom.
B	attracts many protesters.
C	is still popular throughout Spain.

☐

(1 mark)

(d) The siesta …

A	is taken only by the elderly.
B	is needed because of the heat.
C	is becoming popular in Northern Europe.

☐

(1 mark)

Customs

> Guided

2 Look at the photo and make any notes you wish. You will be asked the following three questions and then **two more questions** which you have not prepared.

- ¿Qué hay en la foto?

- ¿Qué costumbre has celebrado en tu casa en el último año?

- ¿Qué tipo de comida prefieres para una ocasión especial?

> Prepare your answers using the prompts. Then listen to the recording of the teacher's questions and answer in the pauses. There is a recording of one student's answers in the answer section to give you more ideas.

¿Qué hay en la foto?

Hay una familia al aire libre alrededor de un fuego porque es el cinco de noviembre, que es una fiesta en Gran Bretaña. Hay fuegos artificiales y un ambiente alegre.

Spanish festivals

A religious festival

1 Read the description of a Spanish religious festival.

Answer the questions in **English**.

bahía = bay

> En muchos pueblos de la costa, la Virgen del Carmen tiene un significado especial porque es la santa patrona de los pescadores y los marineros. Además, en Málaga, se dice que la Virgen también se encarga de cuidar a todos los que se asocian con el mar, hasta a los que nadan o hacen windsurf. El dieciséis de julio, la gente del pueblo lleva la estatua de la Virgen al puerto. Allí la ponen en un barco decorado con luces y flores. Luego la Virgen da una vuelta por la bahía* en el barco, acompañada de música y una procesión de otros barcos.

Example: What is the special significance of the *Virgen del Carmen* for fishermen and sailors? She is their patron saint.

(a) What else do the people of Málaga believe about the *Virgen del Carmen*?

....

.... **(1 mark)**

(b) Where do the villagers first take the statue of the Virgin?

.... **(1 mark)**

(c) Where is the statue then placed? Give full details.

.... **(1 mark)**

(d) Where is the figure taken next?

.... **(1 mark)**

(e) What accompaniment is provided?

.... **(1 mark)**

> Look for key vocabulary in the questions that will guide you to the answer in the text. In question (e), the word 'accompaniment' should direct you to *acompañada* in the text.

A historical festival

2 Cristina is talking about a festival in her home town, Alcoy: 'Los *Moros y los Cristianos'.

los Moros = the Moors (people from North Africa)

What does she say about the festival?

A	People wear traditional dress.
B	There is a re-enactment of a historic battle.
C	The festival commemorates a battle from 80 years ago.
D	The Moors seize the castle from the Christians.
E	The locals are happy to cover the cost of the festival.
F	The festival attracts people from home and abroad.
G	The noise can be excessive at times.
H	People are considerate and don't leave litter behind.

Write the correct letters in the boxes.

Example: A ☐ ☐ ☐ **(3 marks)**

South American festivals

Una fiesta argentina

1 Estás en una sala de chat donde unos jóvenes hablan de las fiestas en los pueblos donde viven. Lee lo que dicen.

Ángela	Para mí lo mejor de todo es el ambiente animado en las calles. Los días de fiesta son muy divertidos.
Lucía	Lo que más me gusta es la cena especial que tenemos en casa para celebrar la ocasión.
Carmen	A mí me encanta la ropa tradicional que la gente se pone cuando hay fiesta.
Eduardo	Para mí lo más emocionante son los fuegos artificiales que empiezan a medianoche.
Felipe	Me gustan más que nada los platos típicos que todo el mundo prepara para la fiesta.

¿Cuál es el aspecto favorito de la fiesta para estos jóvenes? Contesta las preguntas en **español**.

Ejemplo: Ángela   *ambiente animado*

(a)   Lucía   ....   **(1 mark)**

(b)   Carmen   ....   **(1 mark)**

(c)   Eduardo   ....   **(1 mark)**

(d)   Felipe   ....   **(1 mark)**

Una fiesta boliviana

2 Tu amiga Rosalía habla contigo de una fiesta en su país.

¿De qué aspectos de la fiesta habla Rosalía?

Listen to the recording

A	la música
B	la fecha
C	la comida
D	el alojamiento
E	las procesiones
F	la historia
G	los disfraces
H	los visitantes

Escribe las letras correctas en las casillas.

☐ ☐ ☐ ☐

(4 marks)

Describing a region

Granada

Listen to the recording

1   Listen to your teacher talking about the region that you will be visiting during a trip to Spain.

What aspects of the region does the teacher mention?

A	a farm
B	the rivers
C	the coast
D	fishing villages
E	a castle
F	the city
G	the mountains

Write the correct letters in the boxes.

Example

☐ C ☐ ☐ ☐

(3 marks)

Role play: the area where I live

> Prepare your answers using the prompts. Then listen to the recording of the teacher's part and answer in the pauses. If you need more time, simply pause the recording. An example of a complete role play is recorded in the answer section.

Listen to the recording

2   You are talking to your Spanish friend about where you live. The teacher will play the part of your friend and will speak first.

You must address your friend as *tú*. You will talk to the teacher using the five prompts below.

Estás hablando con tu amigo/a español/a sobre dónde vives.

1   Tu ciudad – descripción (**dos** detalles)

2   Historia de tu región (**un** detalle)

3   !

4   Industria de tu región (**dos** detalles)

5   ? Ciudad – número de habitantes

> Listen carefully to the question you are being asked. It is fine to ask your teacher to repeat the question, twice at the most. To do so, you can say: ¿Puedes repetirlo? (Can you repeat it?) or Más despacio, por favor (More slowly please).

Describing a town

Arriving in Sintra

1 Read this extract, adapted from *El Club Dumas* by Arturo Pérez Reverte.

> Corso estuvo en Lisboa menos de cincuenta minutos; el tiempo justo para ir de la estación de Santa Apolonia a la del Rossío. Hora y media más tarde pisaba el andén de Sintra bajo un cielo de nubes bajas que iluminaban las melancólicas torres grises del castillo Da Pena. No había taxis a la vista, y subió andando hasta el pequeño hotel situado enfrente de las dos grandes chimeneas del Palacio Nacional. Eran las diez de la mañana de un miércoles y la explanada estaba libre de turistas y autocares; no hubo problema en conseguir una habitación con vistas al paisaje verde y las mansiones con sus jardines centenarios cubiertas de hiedra.*

*hiedra = ivy

Write the correct letters in the boxes.

Example: What did Corso do in Lisbon?

A	visited Santa Apolonia church
B	went from one station to the other
C	spent time with his friend Rossío

(a) What building did he see on arrival in Sintra?

A	the church towers
B	the Da Pena castle
C	the grey town hall roof

☐

(b) Why did he walk to the hotel?

A	The taxis were all busy.
B	He could not afford a taxi.
C	There were no taxis around.

☐

(c) Where was the hotel?

A	opposite the National Palace
B	next to the National Palace
C	behind the National Palace

☐

(d) What did Corso notice about the esplanade?

A	It was full of people.
B	There were coaches parked along it.
C	It was fairly deserted.

☐

(e) What could he see from his hotel window?

A	old ivy-covered buildings
B	ivy-filled gardens
D	a flower park

☐

(5 marks)

> There will be challenging questions on the Higher exam paper, like this literary extract, but don't be put off by the vocabulary that you don't know. You can gauge the overall meaning from the words that you do recognise and this is often enough to guide you to the correct answer.

Describing your town

2 Tu profesor te ha pedido escribir una descripción de la ciudad para la revista del instituto.

Escribe la descripción en una hoja de papel.

Menciona:

- algo sobre la historia de tu ciudad
- la industria de hoy y dónde trabaja la gente
- los cambios que te gustaría ver en tu ciudad
- los espacios verdes.

Escribe aproximadamente **90** palabras en **español**.   **(16 marks)**

Places to see

What to see in town

1 The woman in the tourist office is explaining what to see in the town.

Listen to the recording and answer the following questions in **English**.

Example: What is the best thing about the town? *the combination of old and new*

Listen to the recording

(a) Where is the medieval castle? Give **two exact** details.

....

.... **(2 marks)**

(b) Why is the bullring particularly interesting?

.... **(1 mark)**

(c) How do we know the museum is award-winning?

.... **(1 mark)**

(d) What does the museum show?

.... **(1 mark)**

(e) Where is the modern art gallery?

.... **(1 mark)**

(f) Where is the chemist?

.... **(1 mark)**

> If the question asks you to give details / exact details, you must produce a full answer. For example, if you hear *El museo está en la Plaza Mayor al lado de la biblioteca* and are asked to give exact details, you should write 'the museum is in the main square next to the library'.

Places to see

2 Look at the photo and make any notes you wish. You will be asked the following three questions and then **two more questions** which you have not prepared.

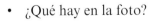
Listen to the recording

- ¿Qué hay en la foto?

- ¿Qué ciudades piensas visitar en otros países?

- ¿Qué visitaste en tus últimas vacaciones?

> Prepare your answers using the prompts. Then listen to the recording of the teacher's questions and answer in the pauses. There is a recording of one student's answers in the answer section to give you more ideas.

Had a go ☐ **Nearly there** ☐ **Nailed it!** ☐

Places to visit

Listen to the recording

What to visit

1 You ask the receptionist at your hotel about what to see in the area.

What does he say? Write the correct answer in each box.

Example: The weather is going to be …

A	dull and cloudy.
B	chilly.
C	ideal for sightseeing.

☐ C

(a) In Oviedo he recommends …

A	the modern shopping streets.
B	the historic areas.
C	the old market and statues.

☐

(1 mark)

(b) Gijón is …

A	an expensive town.
B	a walled city.
C	on the coast.

☐

(1 mark)

(c) When you arrive in Avilés, it seems …

A	quite ugly.
B	very quiet.
C	extremely modern.

☐

(1 mark)

(d) Proaza is great for …

A	hiring quad bikes.
B	watching the cycling race.
C	a country bike ride.

☐

(1 mark)

(e) El Nalón is a good place for …

A	walks by the river.
B	river-side cafés.
C	canoeing.

☐

(1 mark)

Mi ciudad

2 Tu compañero de intercambio español pregunta lo que se puede hacer en tu región.

Escribe un correo electrónico a tu amigo.

Menciona:

- lo que hay en tu ciudad
- unas actividades que vais a hacer durante el día
- lo que se puede hacer por la noche
- una visita que hiciste recientemente en tu región.

Escribe aproximadamente **90** palabras en **español**.

> Always read the tasks in full before you start, so that you can plan what you are going to write. This way you will not end up repeating yourself and will use a greater variety of language.

....

....

....

....

....

....

.... **(16 marks)**

The weather

El pronóstico del tiempo

1   Lee este boletín para varias partes de España.

A	**Albacete:** habrá temperaturas altas durante todo el día con la posibilidad de tormentas esta tarde con lluvias intensas en algunas zonas.
B	**Barcelona:** un día caluroso y soleado para todos, con temperaturas elevadas para la estación. El buen tiempo continuará varios días.
C	**Cartagena:** no hace frío, pero será un día nublado con cielos cubiertos en todas partes. Posibilidades de niebla en zonas junto al mar.
D	**Denia:** seco, pero con vientos fuertes en algunas zonas. Temperaturas bajas todo el día.

¿Dónde viven estas personas?

Escribe la letra correcta en cada casilla.

Ejemplo: Los truenos me dan miedo.   `A`

(a)   Es perfecto para el windsurf.   ☐   **(1 mark)**

(b)   Me pongo abrigo y guantes.   ☐   **(1 mark)**

(c)   Ideal para nadar en el mar.   ☐   **(1 mark)**

(d)   Voy a llevar el paraguas.   ☐   **(1 mark)**

(e)   No conduciré en la carretera de la costa.   ☐   **(1 mark)**

El clima del norte

2   Translate this passage into **English**.

> Vivo en el noroeste de España y el clima aquí no es tan caluroso como en el sur. En verano hace buen tiempo con temperaturas agradables, pero el sol no brilla todos los días. Hemos tenido un fin de semana lluvioso y mañana hará bastante viento.

....

....

....

....

....

....   **(9 marks)**

> When you are translating, remember that you cannot always translate word for word, as it will produce some very odd-sounding English. Translating *todos los días* literally would produce 'all the days', so you need to think for a moment and come up with a natural phrase such as 'every day'.

Shopping

Shopping trends

1 Read these comments about shopping on an online forum.

> No entiendo por qué a la gente le gusta ir de compras. Yo prefiero quedarme en casa y buscar ofertas y descuentos en línea. A veces, sin embargo, compro cositas en la tienda que está al lado de mi casa porque es más práctico. Así evito la ciudad, que está siempre muy concurrida. **Mónica**
>
> Normalmente compro en las tiendas de uno de los centros comerciales que hay en la ciudad. Me encanta la variedad y los productos suelen ser bastante baratos. Nunca voy a las tiendas en mi pueblo porque los precios son altísimos, pero a veces compro en la red. **Eduardo**

Who expresses the following opinions?

Write **M** for **Mónica**   **E** for **Eduardo**   **M+E** for **Mónica and Eduardo**

Example: I shop from home.   ☐ M

(a) I sometimes shop locally.   ☐   **(1 mark)**

(b) I go to the city to do my shopping.   ☐   **(1 mark)**

(c) I take costs into account.   ☐   **(1 mark)**

(d) I shop online.   ☐   **(1 mark)**

Shopping preferences

2 Listen to four people discussing their shopping preferences. Answer the questions in **English**.

Example: What does Pablo say about where he prefers to shop? He doesn't mind

(a) Why doesn't Ana like the shops in her neighbourhood?

.... **(1 mark)**

(b) What **two** things does Inés do instead of buying things?

....

.... **(2 marks)**

(c) How does Ricardo prefer to shop?

.... **(1 mark)**

Listen to the recording

Role play: shopping

3 While on an exchange visit to Spain, your exchange partner, Camila, asks what you would like to do. The teacher will play the role of Camila and will speak first.

You must address Camila as *tú*. You will talk to the teacher using the five prompts below. Listen to the recording and answer in the pauses.

Estás con tu amiga española y te pregunta qué quieres hacer.

Listen to the recording

1 Ir de compras – tu razón   4 !

2 Dónde y tu razón   5 **?** Opinión sobre ir de compras

3 Cosas para comprar (**dos** detalles)

Buying gifts

Shopping for presents

1   Listen to your Spanish friend, Pablo, and his sister, Laura, talking while you are shopping.

Write the correct letter in each box.

(a) Where does Pablo recommend they should go?

A	supermarket
B	market
C	shopping centre

☐ **(1 mark)**

(b) What is the **main** reason that Pablo wants to go there?

A	It is nearby.
B	It has good variety.
C	It is cheaper.

☐ **(1 mark)**

(c) What special event are they buying for?

A	birthday
B	anniversary
C	Christmas

☐ **(1 mark)**

(d) What does Laura think they should buy?

A	clothes
B	jewellery
C	perfume

☐ **(1 mark)**

(e) In what circumstances might they buy a book?

A	If they see a good one.
B	If they have money left.
C	If the novel they want is in the shops.

☐ **(1 mark)**

Wrapping gifts

2   Your Spanish exchange partner's mother has left instructions for you both to wrap and label some Christmas presents for her nieces. Read the note.

Which present is for each person? Write the correct letter in each box.

A	Los guantes rojos y el monedero de piel son para Ángela.
B	El cinturón de cuero y los vaqueros negros son para Bárbara.
C	Las zapatillas de deporte y el jersey de lana son para Claudia.
D	El paraguas azul y el collar verde son para Daniela.

(a) Something made of wool   ☐   **(1 mark)**

(b) A belt   ☐   **(1 mark)**

(c) Some jewellery   ☐   **(1 mark)**

(d) A useful gift for rainy weather   ☐   **(1 mark)**

(e) Some gloves   ☐   **(1 mark)**

(f) Some footwear   ☐   **(1 mark)**

Money

Young people and money

1 Read the article below.

Los resultados indican que cerca del 70% de los menores y adolescentes reciben su paga en efectivo* para que realicen sus propias compras. Este dinero lo obtienen de sus padres en la mayoría de los casos, pero también de otros familiares.

"Esto sugiere que hay hogares en los cuales los niños reciben dinero de varias fuentes, lo cual ha aumentado en más del 50% la cantidad que reciben en comparación con otros tiempos", señaló Leonardo Ortegón, uno de los autores del estudio.

Según la investigación, los productos en los que más invierten su dinero son: las actividades de entretenimiento (22%), los alimentos y bebidas (21%) y los servicios de comunicación de telefonía celular (19%) e Internet (18%).

El estudio, además, concluye que el gasto per cápita por niño ha aumentado en las familias bogotanas**. Los padres y especialmente los abuelos están comprando más productos para sus hijos, en parte debido a que tienen mayores ingresos para gastar en estos artículos, pero también porque son presionados por ellos mismos para aumentar su consumo.

*efectivo = cash
**bogotanas = from Bogotá, the capital of Colombia

Answer the following questions in **English**.

Example: Why do young people get paid in cash? So they can make their own purchases

(a) From whom do young people receive their pocket money?

.... **(1 mark)**

(b) What is said about the amount they receive?

.... **(1 mark)**

(c) What do they spend the largest percentage of their money on?

.... **(1 mark)**

(d) What spending has gone up in families?

.... **(1 mark)**

(e) Give one reason why this is happening.

.... **(1 mark)**

Role play: talking about money

2 You are talking to your Spanish exchange partner about money. The teacher will play the role of your exchange partner and will speak first.

You must address your partner as *tú*. You will talk to the teacher using the five prompts below.

Estás hablando con tu amigo/a sobre el dinero.

1 Paga – cuánto

2 Paga – de quién y cuándo

3 !

4 Dinero – tus gastos (**dos** detalles)

5 ? Paga – bastante

Listen to the recording

Prepare your answers using the prompts. Then listen to the recording of the teacher's part and answer in the pauses. If you need more time, simply pause the recording. An example of a complete role play is recorded in the answer section.

Remember that asking Spanish questions is easy. To ask the question 'Do you receive enough pocket money?' you just say 'you receive' (*recibes*), add the words for 'enough' and 'money' and put a questioning tone into your voice by making it go up at the end.

Local, national,
international and global
areas of interest

Charities

Charity events

1 You are at your Spanish penfriend's school, listening to a report from the head of the student charity group.

What does she say?

Listen to the recording and write the correct letter in each box.

Listen to the
recording

(a) They organised a charity disco …

A	for their schoolmates.
B	at Christmas.
C	in a primary school.

☐

(b) They raised eighty euros …

A	for orphaned children.
B	for endangered wildlife.
C	for homeless pets.

☐

(c) The Christmas event …

A	took place at the hospital.
B	was a competition for parents.
C	involved nine teams.

☐

(d) The cakes …

A	went on sale at break.
B	were on a stall at the summer fete.
C	were a bit expensive to make.

☐

(e) The environmental charity received a cheque for …

A	50 euros.
B	100 euros.
C	150 euros.

☐

(f) For the children's charity they will be collecting …

A	things to wear.
B	things to eat.
C	things to play with.

☐

(6 marks)

Role play: charity events

> Guided

2 You are talking to your Spanish friend, who has asked what charity events your school organises.

The teacher will play the part of your friend and will speak first.

> Prepare your answers using the prompts. Then listen to the recording of the teacher's part and answer in the pauses. If you need more time, simply pause the recording. An example of a complete role play is recorded in the answer section.

Listen to the
recording

You must address your friend as *tú*. You will talk to the teacher using the five prompts below.

Estás hablando con tu amigo/a sobre los eventos benéficos en tu instituto.

1   Asociaciones – cuáles

2   Actividades – descripción

3   **!**

4   Beneficio para el individuo – **un** detalle

5   **?** Organización benéfica favorita – **una** razón

> You might not always be able to tell the truth in these exercises! Here, perhaps your school doesn't get involved in charity events or you can't remember. Your aim is to show off your knowledge of Spanish so, as long as your answer is reasonable (for example, you wouldn't claim to have made a million euros from a cake sale!), that is fine. You can get inspiration from exercise 1 or from the Revision Guide.

Volunteering

Reasons to volunteer

1 Read what these young people say about why you should volunteer.

A "Simplemente para ayudar a los más necesitados. Seguramente sea la primera razón por la que la gente hace trabajo voluntario, pero no es la única." **Alex**

B "Refuerza la autoestima. No solo te sientes bien ayudando a los demás. También las personas a las que ayudas o los compañeros que conoces te valoran por tu esfuerzo." **Begoña**

C "Para cuidar el medioambiente. No solo existe voluntariado para ayudar a personas, también hay para proteger a la naturaleza." **Carlos**

D "Aprender a relacionarte. En el voluntariado conocerás a gente nueva, y si tienes problemas con las relaciones personales, te ayudará a abrirte a los demás. Aprenderás a trabajar eficazmente en grupo." **Daniela**

Who says what about volunteering?

Write the correct letter in each box.

(a) Who talks about assisting people less fortunate than ourselves? ☐ **(1 mark)**

(b) Who states that you can get involved in helping wildlife? ☐ **(1 mark)**

(c) Who suggests you can improve interpersonal skills? ☐ **(1 mark)**

(d) Who mentions how you will feel about yourself? ☐ **(1 mark)**

(e) Who outlines the benefits in developing your team work? ☐ **(1 mark)**

Topic: Volunteering

2 Look at the photo and make any notes you wish. You will be asked the following three questions and then **two more questions** which you have not prepared.

- ¿Qué hay en la foto?

- ¿Cuáles son los beneficios del trabajo voluntario?

- ¿Qué experiencia de trabajo voluntario has tenido?

Listen to the recording

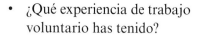

Prepare your answers using the prompts. Then listen to the recording of the teacher's questions and answer in the pauses. There is a recording of one student's answers in the answer section to give you more ideas.

Helping others

Helping friends

1 Listen to some Spanish friends talking about how they have helped friends. How did they help?

A	Lending money
B	Helping with a get-fit routine
C	Solving romantic problems
D	Intervening in a bullying issue
E	Doing a repair job
F	Helping with studies
G	Giving a lift
H	Supporting after a family break-up

Write the correct letter in each box.

(a) Miguel ☐　　　　　　　　　　　　　　　　　　　**(1 mark)**

(b) Sandra ☐　　　　　　　　　　　　　　　　　　　**(1 mark)**

(c) David ☐　　　　　　　　　　　　　　　　　　　**(1 mark)**

(d) Paula ☐　　　　　　　　　　　　　　　　　　　**(1 mark)**

Helping at home

2 Publicas esta foto para tus amigos en tu página de una red social.

Escribe **cuatro** frases en **español** que describan la foto.

1 .... **(2 marks)**

2 .... **(2 marks)**

3 .... **(2 marks)**

4 .... **(2 marks)**

Healthy living

Manolo's experience

1   Read this letter in a Spanish magazine.

> Debido a un cambio radical en mi estilo de vida y en mi dieta diaria, he podido perder bastantes kilos y me siento muchísimo mejor porque hoy tengo el peso que quiero tener. De niño, tenía un apetito insaciable para los caramelos y el chocolate. Evitaba los platos principales de la cena porque solo me interesaba el postre. Como consecuencia, siempre fui gordito y los otros niños se reían de mí. Ahora, para mantener esta delgadez, he decidido que necesito hacer ejercicio. El único deporte que me atrae es el piragüismo y estoy muy emocionado porque tengo mi primera sesión en el río mañana.
>
> **Manolo**

Which stages of Manolo's life do the following situations apply to?

Write **P** for something that happened in the **past**.

Write **N** for something that is happening **now**.

Write **F** for something that is going to happen in the **future**.

Write the correct letter in each box.

(a) Having canoeing lessons   ☐   **(1 mark)**

(b) Eating sweet things   ☐   **(1 mark)**

(c) Achieving the ideal weight   ☐   **(1 mark)**

(d) Being laughed at   ☐   **(1 mark)**

Eating healthily

2   Your Spanish friends are trying to eat more healthily and are talking about what they ate the previous day. What did each one have? Answer in **English**.

Example: salad with tuna

Listen to the recording

(a) .... with .... **(2 marks)**

(b) .... with .... **(2 marks)**

(c) .... with .... **(2 marks)**

Unhealthy living

An unhealthy trend

1 Read this article in a Spanish magazine.

> Es viernes, las diez de la noche, y en un parque en Vigo los jóvenes se están empezando a congregar. Llegan con bolsas de plástico y se reúnen en grupos de seis a diez. De las bolsas sacan botellas, vasos y paquetes. Se sirven cócteles de vino tinto y coca cola (llamados 'calimocho') y comen patatas fritas. En todo el parque debe haber más de cien adolescentes y todos tienen la intención de emborracharse. Columnas de humo se levantan de cada grupo y por el olor se sabe que no es tabaco normal sino porro. Aparte del daño que se hacen a sí mismos, estos jóvenes también molestan a los vecinos que se quejan del ruido y la basura. Las autoridades intentan prohibir el botellón, pero cada fin de semana reaparecen en otro lugar para fastidiar a otro grupo de vecinos.

Answer the questions in **English**.

(a) What are the young people carrying in the bags?

.... **(1 mark)**

(b) What is a *calimocho*?

.... **(1 mark)**

(c) What is the aim of the young people who gather there?

.... **(1 mark)**

(d) What does the author conclude from the smell?

.... **(1 mark)**

(e) What do the neighbours complain about?

.... **(1 mark)**

(f) Has the ban affected the *botellón*? Explain your answer.

.... **(1 mark)**

Translation

2 Translate the following sentences into **Spanish**.

(a) Young people must never smoke.

....

(b) You should resist the temptation to take drugs.

....

(c) I have to look after my heart.

....

(d) My brother should lose a few pounds.

....

(e) My parents only drink alcohol in moderation.

.... **(10 marks)**

Peer group pressure

A dreadful year

1 Read this story about a teenage girl's experience.

> Soy Natalia y siempre he sido una chica un poco atrevida, pero el año pasado tomé unas decisiones muy estúpidas. Dejé de ver a mi mejor amiga, Sara, y empecé a salir con un grupo de chicos muy rebeldes. Pensé que eran emocionantes y animados, pero en realidad eran desagradables. Bajo su influencia comencé a hacer cosas estúpidas como fumar y beber alcohol y, en varias ocasiones, tomé drogas. Mis notas en el instituto bajaron y empecé a robar a mis padres para tener más dinero.
> Un día, Sara vino a la casa y, convencida de que podría ayudarme, me mostró fotos de los días de antes cuando íbamos de compras juntas o salíamos al cine. Fue entonces cuando entendí la verdad de los riesgos que corría con este estilo de vida y decidí abandonar ese grupo de idiotas. ¡Y lo hice! Ahora soy una persona muy distinta, pero Sara es todavía mi mejor amiga.

Which adjectives describe each person or thing?

A	foolish
B	exciting
C	unpleasant

D	dishonest
E	optimistic
F	positive

G	different
H	daring

I	brave
J	negative

Write the correct letter in each box.

(a) What Natalia has always been like ☐

(b) Natalia's decisions last year ☐

(c) How her new friends seemed ☐

(d) What her new friends were really like ☐

(e) Her friends' influence ☐

(f) What Natalia is like now ☐

(6 marks)

Un artículo sobre los amigos

2 Decides escribir un artículo sobre los amigos para la revista española de tu instituto.

Menciona:

- una descripción de tu amigo/a
- los problemas causados por la presión de grupo
- tus planes para el próximo fin de semana con tu amigo/a.

Escribe aproximadamente **90** palabras en **español**.

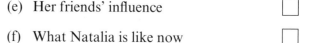

....

....

....

....

....

....

.... **(16 marks)**

Green issues

Campañas medioambientales

1 Lee este artículo sobre unas iniciativas verdes.

A **Campaña Planeta**
Trabajamos con las especies amenazadas para protegerlas y para conseguir que tengan un futuro más seguro. Visitamos centros de enseñanza para hacer presentaciones sobre las causas de su desaparición.

B **Campaña Mundo**
Nuestros científicos siguen buscando maneras de canalizar las fuerzas naturales del viento y del sol para reemplazar el uso tradicional de combustibles fósiles.

C **Campaña Tierra**
Nuestro grupo trabaja sin cesar para proteger las zonas salvajes de nuestro planeta como selvas tropicales y bosques antiguos. Estas zonas son los pulmones de nuestra tierra.

D **Campaña Global**
Nuestro equipo investiga fábricas y empresas que no cumplen con las leyes de seguridad y limpieza; y de esta forma contaminan los ríos, el aire y la tierra a su alrededor.

¿Qué campaña corresponde a cada frase?

Escribe la letra correcta en cada casilla.

> With questions all in Spanish, you will often need to look out for synonyms, and it is worthwhile learning some. For example: *planeta, mundo, tierra* (planet, world, earth); *viejo, antiguo, anciano* (old); *bosque, árboles, selva* (wood, trees, forest).

(a) Nuestro objetivo es la protección de los animales. ☐ **(1 mark)**

(b) Intentamos evitar que corten los árboles. ☐ **(1 mark)**

(c) Nos aseguramos de que las industrias no polucionen. ☐ **(1 mark)**

(d) Investigamos las fuentes de energía alternativas. ☐ **(1 mark)**

(e) Intentamos interesar a los estudiantes en nuestra causa. ☐ **(1 mark)**

(f) Obligamos a las compañías a cumplir con la legislación. ☐ **(1 mark)**

Climate change

2 You are in a geography class in your Spanish friend's school listening to a talk about climate change.

What issues are mentioned?

Listen to the recording

A	earthquakes
B	heavy rains
C	floods
D	desertification
E	hurricanes
F	drought
G	spread of disease
H	global warming

Write the correct letters in the boxes.

☐ ☐ ☐ ☐

(4 marks)

Had a go ☐ **Nearly there** ☐ **Nailed it!** ☐

Natural resources

Saving resources

Listen to the recording

1 Listen to your Spanish friends discuss saving resources.

Choose the correct ending for each sentence. Write the correct letter in each box.

(a) María thinks a good idea was …

A	charging for bags in shops.
B	recycling plastic bags.
C	reducing packaging in supermarkets.

☐

(b) The statistics show that …

A	7% more people are reusing plastic bags.
B	use of plastic bags has gone down 17%.
C	the use of cloth bags went up 70%.

☐

(c) Tomás and his family …

A	turn left-over food into compost.
B	tend to waste a lot of food.
C	use up leftovers creatively.

☐

(d) Eva and her family …

A	grow a lot of their own food.
B	sell organic produce on the market.
C	use only natural pesticides.

☐

(e) Ricardo's father …

A	has installed solar panels.
B	is going to install solar panels.
C	is currently installing solar panels.

☐

(f) Ricardo's father is considering a generator …

A	that uses less electricity.
B	driven by the wind.
C	powered by the sun.

☐

(6 marks)

Topic: Protecting the environment

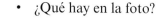

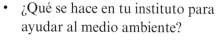

Listen to the recording

2 Look at the photo and make any notes you wish. You will be asked the following three questions and then **two more questions** which you have not prepared.

- ¿Qué hay en la foto?

- ¿Qué se hace en tu instituto para ayudar al medio ambiente?

- ¿Qué has reciclado en casa el mes pasado?

> Prepare your answers using the prompts. Then listen to the recording of the teacher's questions and answer in the pauses. There is a recording of one student's answers in the answer section to give you more ideas.

:

Environmental action

Supporting campaigns

1   Read these opinions on a school forum about which initiative the school should support.

A	Lo mejor sería trabajar para reducir la cantidad de electricidad que se usa en el colegio. Si apagamos las luces y los ordenadores al final del día, ahorraremos mucho. **José**
B	En mi opinión, deberíamos hacer algo con la enorme cantidad de papel y cartón que tiramos a la basura. Estoy segura que podríamos llevarlo a una empresa de reciclaje. **Ana**
C	Yo recomiendo un día sin coches para reducir la cantidad de gasolina usada y de gases emitidos. Hay muchos estudiantes que no necesitan usar el transporte para llegar al colegio. **Miguel**
D	Deberíamos organizar un grupo para ayudar a limpiar zonas sucias en el barrio. El río está muy contaminado con basura y los peces están amenazados. **Pilar**

Who expresses the following opinions?

Write the correct letter in each box.

(a) I recommend a day of walking or cycling to school.   ☐   **(1 mark)**

(b) I think they need to cut down on electricity usage.   ☐   **(1 mark)**

(c) I would like to use the services of a recycling company.   ☐   **(1 mark)**

(e) I suggest cleaning up polluted areas nearby.   ☐   **(1 mark)**

(f) I would like to prioritise cleaner air.   ☐   **(1 mark)**

(g) I think we should try to save energy.   ☐   **(1 mark)**

> The topic of the environment is not as challenging as you might expect, because many of the words are very similar in both languages. Note this key vocabulary: *electricidad* – electricity, *energía* – energy, *contaminación* – contamination/pollution, *reciclar* – to recycle.

Sea pollution

2   Listen to your Spanish friend, who is telling you about an initiative she has heard of.

Answer the following questions in **English**.

Example: Where did she learn about the initiative? *a television programme*

(a) What skill did the young people use? ....   **(1 mark)**

(b) What are they trying to protect? ....   **(1 mark)**

(c) Which **two** groups of people are to blame for the pollution?

....   **(2 marks)**

(d) What are the **two** worst types of pollution?

....   **(2 marks)**

(e) What is the fate of some fish? ....   **(1 mark)**

Global issues

Poverty

1 Read this extract adapted from *Réquiem por un campesino español* by Ramón J. Sender.

Paco, an altar boy, has just visited a sick man with the priest, Mosén Millán.

> —¿Esa gente es la más pobre del pueblo, Mosén Millán?
> —Quién sabe, pero hay cosas peores que la pobreza. Son desgraciados por otras razones.
> El monaguillo* veía que el sacerdote** contestaba con desgana.
> —¿Por qué? —preguntó.
> —Tienen un hijo que podría ayudarles, pero he oído decir que está en la cárcel***.
> —¿Ha matado**** a alguno?
> —Yo no sé, pero no me extrañaría.
> Paco no podía estar callado. Caminaba a oscuras por terreno desigual. Recordando al enfermo el monaguillo dijo: —Se está muriendo porque no puede respirar. Y ahora nos vamos, y se queda allí solo.

monaguillo = altar boy   **sacerdote* = priest   ****cárcel* = prison   *****matar* = to kill

Answer the following questions in **English.**

(a) What does Paco want to know about the people?

.... **(1 mark)**

(b) What does Mosén Millán say about poverty?

.... **(1 mark)**

(c) Why can't the son help his parents?

.... **(1 mark)**

(d) What does Paco want to know about the son?

.... **(1 mark)**

(e) What does Paco think is going to happen to the sick man?

.... **(1 mark)**

(f) What does he feel guilty about at the end?

.... **(1 mark)**

Concerns about global issues

2 You are in a Spanish school listening to a discussion about global issues. What issue concerns each student? Write the correct letter in each box.

A	natural disasters	D	poverty	G	world hunger
B	world peace	E	homelessness	H	environmental damage
C	human rights	F	unemployment		

Listen to the recording

(a) Inés ☐ **(1 mark)**   (c) Cristina ☐ **(1 mark)**

(b) Rafael ☐ **(1 mark)**   (d) Roberto ☐ **(1 mark)**

Had a go ☐ Nearly there ☐ Nailed it! ☐

Local, national,
international and global
areas of interest

Poverty

Poverty in Puerto Rico

1   Read this article about poverty among children and young people in an online newspaper.

● ● ●

> El sociólogo Carlos Quintana ha hecho un estudio sobre la pobreza en Puerto Rico y declara que el 84% de los niños vive en condiciones de extrema pobreza. La mitad de estos niños tiene padres desempleados y el paro en la isla va de mal en peor. El 59% de los niños vive en hogares monoparentales y el 15% de los adolescentes ni va a la escuela ni trabaja. El 11% de los bebés tiene bajo peso al nacer, mientras que en Estados Unidos esta cifra se reduce al 8%.

Which group of children or young people does each figure refer to?

A	They come from single-parent families.
B	They have unemployed parents.
C	They live on the streets.
D	They have low birth weight.
E	They live in extreme poverty.
F	They are orphans.
G	They are sent out to work too young.
H	They neither work nor study.

Write the correct letter in each box.

(a) 84%   ☐   **(1 mark)**

(b) 50%   ☐   **(1 mark)**

(c) 59%   ☐   **(1 mark)**

(d) 15%   ☐   **(1 mark)**

(e) 11%   ☐   **(1 mark)**

Translation

2   Translate the following passage into **Spanish**.

> It worries me that there is so much poverty in my country. There are many children who do not have enough to eat. They live in houses without heating and in winter they go cold and hungry. This Christmas, in my class, we are going to collect blankets and food to take to needy families. Yesterday I took some tins and packets to school.

....

....

....

....

....

....   **(9 marks)**

Had a go ☐ Nearly there ☐ Nailed it! ☐

Homelessness

Listen to the recording

Helping in a hostel

1 You are with your Spanish friend who is starting voluntary work at a hostel for the homeless. Listen to the hostel manager explaining their work and write the correct letter in each box.

(a) How long can people stay at the hostel?

A	The maximum is always two nights.
B	It depends on their health.
C	Each case is considered individually.

☐ **(1 mark)**

(b) What does she say about clothes?

A	The residents have their clothes washed at the hostel.
B	Charity shops donate clothes to the hostel.
C	Residents are given a set of clean clothes on arrival.

☐ **(1 mark)**

(c) What does she say about food?

A	The homeless can come for a meal three times a week.
B	They get food vouchers to spend in the supermarkets.
C	Local shops donate unsold food to the hostel.

☐ **(1 mark)**

(d) What statistic is given about homeless people?

A	Ninety per cent of homeless people are male.
B	One in ten of the current residents are women.
C	A small number of homeless people are couples.

☐ **(1 mark)**

Topic: Homelessness

Listen to the recording

2 Look at the photo and make any notes you wish. You will be asked the following three questions and then **two more questions** which you have not prepared.

- ¿Qué hay en la foto?

- ¿Cuál sería el regalo ideal para un hombre sin techo?

- ¿Cuál es el problema principal para las personas sin techo?

Prepare your answers using the prompts. Then listen to the recording of the teacher's questions and answer in the pauses. There is a recording of one student's answers in the answer section to give you more ideas.

Countries and nationalities

Visiting tourists

1   Read this report about last year's tourism figures in Valencia.

Write the correct letter in each box.

A	Belgian
B	Danish
C	Dutch
D	European
E	Foreign
F	German
G	Greek
H	Spanish
I	Swedish

La mayoría de los turistas fueron visitantes nacionales de otras comunidades españolas, pero hemos visto un mayor número de otros viajeros europeos que en los años anteriores. La región es popular con los holandeses, pero nunca atrae a muchos daneses. No vinieron tantos alemanes como antes, pero había más griegos que el año pasado. Los suecos suelen alojarse en el campo a varios kilómetros de la costa, mientras que los belgas siempre optan por hoteles junto a la playa.

> The questions are carefully written to give you clues to where in the text to find your answer. Look out for vocabulary that appears in the question, such as 'majority', which should send you to *mayoría* in the text. Read around the word carefully to find the correct answer. Be wary of negatives, however, because if the text said *la mayoría de los turistas **no** fueron visitantes nacionales*, you would have to look elsewhere for the answer.

(a) What nationality were the majority of visitors?   ☐   **(1 mark)**

(b) Which visitors travelled to the region in greater numbers?   ☐   **(1 mark)**

(c) With which nationality is the region popular?   ☐   **(1 mark)**

(d) Which visitors are not attracted to the region?   ☐   **(1 mark)**

(e) Which nationality's numbers were down compared to previous years?   ☐   **(1 mark)**

(f) Which visitors tend to stay inland?   ☐   **(1 mark)**

(g) Which tourists stay close to the beach?   ☐   **(1 mark)**

At the language school

2   The other students in the language school are introducing themselves. Where are the students from?

Write the correct letter in each box.

Listen to the recording

A	England
B	Canada
C	France
D	Ireland
E	Russia
F	Scotland
G	USA
H	Wales

(a) David   ☐   **(1 mark)**   (c) Andrew   ☐   **(1 mark)**

(b) Susan   ☐   **(1 mark)**   (d) Alex   ☐   **(1 mark)**

49

Tourist information

In the tourist office

1   You hear a conversation between a customer and the assistant in the tourist office.

Listen to the recording and answer the following questions in **English**.

Example: What does the customer ask for? *information about the town*

Listen to the recording

(a) What does the assistant give him?

.... **(1 mark)**

(b) Where is the tourist office situated?

.... **(1 mark)**

(c) Where will he find the shops?

.... **(1 mark)**

(d) What does he learn about the museum?

.... **(1 mark)**

(e) What does the leaflet explain? Give **two exact** details.

....

.... **(2 marks)**

(f) What does the assistant recommend?

.... **(1 mark)**

Role play: enquiries at the tourist office

> Prepare your answers using the prompts. Then listen to the recording of the teacher's part and answer in the pauses. If you need more time, simply pause the recording. An example of a complete role play is recorded in the answer section.

Listen to the recording

2   You are talking to an employee in the tourist office. The teacher will play the part of the employee and will speak first.

You must address the employee as *usted*. You will talk to the teacher using the five prompts below.

Hablas con el empleado / la empleada.

1.   Sitios de interés – información

2.   Alojamiento – lista

3.   **!**

4.   Transporte – horario

5.   **?** Estación – dónde

> Try to vary the language you use. For example, when asking for things you can alternate between *quiero*, *quisiera* and *me gustaría*.

Accommodation

Opinions about accommodation

1 You see these opinions on a website.

A	Me encantan los hoteles. Me gusta no tener que hacer mi cama ni ayudar en nada. Allí hay gente que te lo hace todo. ¡Es genial! **Pili**
B	Me gustan las actividades al aire libre. Soy una persona sencilla y no necesito muchos lujos. **Pablo**
C	Lo que a mí me gusta es poder hacer mis deportes preferidos: hago esquí acuático y me gusta nadar largas distancias. Es muy difícil hacerlos en la ciudad donde vivo. **Marisa**
D	No soy aficionado a las vacaciones en hoteles. Prefiero pasar mis vacaciones en casa de familia y amigos. **Julio**

Write the correct letter in each box.

Who …

> Watch out for negative expressions such as *no … ni.*

(a) likes water sports? ☐ **(1 mark)**

(b) likes a change from doing housework? ☐ **(1 mark)**

(c) doesn't like to be indoors? ☐ **(1 mark)**

(d) prefers to stay in hotels? ☐ **(1 mark)**

(e) is more concerned about who to spend a holiday with? ☐ **(1 mark)**

Where to go

2 Your Spanish friends are talking about where they go on holiday.

Listen to their conversation and answer the following questions in **English**.

Example: Where does Marcelo's family go? flat in Madrid

> Always look at the example to see how much information is required. Here, you need to give the accommodation **and** the location.

Listen to the recording

(a) Where does Paulina always go? .... **(1 mark)**

(b) Where does Rogelio love to go? .... **(1 mark)**

(c) Where does Samuel go with his friends? .... **(1 mark)**

(d) Where does Eva's family always go? .... **(1 mark)**

Hotels

Reservations

1 Read these extracts from hotel bookings.

> ✉
>
> Nos gustaría reservar un apartamento en la planta baja. Tengo movilidad reducida y tengo problemas para subir escaleras.
> **A**

> ✉
>
> Preferimos una habitación en la parte de atrás del hotel, de las que dan al mar, porque en el otro lado, las vistas de las montañas no son tan bonitas.
> **C**

> ✉
>
> Si es posible, queremos una habitación lejos del ascensor porque, según nuestra experiencia, puede ser bastante ruidoso allí con la gente subiendo y bajando.
> **B**

> ✉
>
> Por lo que nos dicen los amigos, no basta con dejar abiertas las ventanas durante la noche. Para dormir hace falta el aire acondicionado.
> **D**

What has each guest specifically mentioned?

Write the correct letter in each box.

(a) A room away from the lift ☐ **(1 mark)**

(b) Keeping cool ☐ **(1 mark)**

(c) Being on the ground floor ☐ **(1 mark)**

(d) Mobility problems ☐ **(1 mark)**

(e) A room at the back ☐ **(1 mark)**

Mr Gómez books a hotel

2 Listen to the recording and answer the following questions in **English**.

(a) Who is Mr Gómez making a reservation for?

.... **(1 mark)**

(b) What are **two** benefits of taking the family room instead of two rooms?

....

.... **(2 marks)**

(c) Which facilities are available in the room?

A	TV
B	internet connection
C	tea/coffee-making facilities
D	fridge

E	phone
F	shower
G	air conditioning
H	balcony

Write the correct letters in the boxes.

☐ ☐ ☐ ☐ **(4 marks)**

(d) How many nights will they be staying?

.... **(1 mark)**

Listen to the recording

Camping

A camping holiday

1 Lucas leaves a voicemail message for Alejandro about their planned camping holiday.

Write the correct letter in each box.

(a) What does Lucas say about the camping equipment?

A	The campsite will have everything they need.
B	They can hire any necessary equipment once they are there.
C	They will need to take everything they need with them.

☐   **(1 mark)**

(b) What does Lucas say about the tent?

A	They will probably need to buy a two-man tent.
B	Lucas has a couple of one-man tents.
C	Two people could fit easily into his tent.

☐   **(1 mark)**

(c) What does Lucas say about the campsite facilities?

A	There are washing facilities.
B	There is a food shop.
C	There is a games room.

☐   **(1 mark)**

(d) What does Lucas say about the location of the campsite?

A	It's on the coast.
B	It's by a river.
C	It's near a mountain lake.

☐   **(1 mark)**

Role play: booking a campsite

> Prepare your answers using the prompts. Then listen to the recording of the teacher's part and answer in the pauses. If you need more time, simply pause the recording. An example of a complete role play is recorded in the answer section.

2 You are phoning a Spanish campsite and want to reserve a pitch *(una parcela)*. The teacher will play the part of the booking clerk and will speak first.

You must address the booking clerk as *usted*. You will talk to the teacher using the five prompts below.

Estás hablando por teléfono con el empleado/la empleada del camping y quieres reservar una parcela.

1   Reserva – número de personas y tiendas

2   Número de noches y fecha de llegada

3   !

4   Una cosa que necesitas alquilar

5   ? Instalaciones en el camping

> When using the formal 'you' *(usted)*, you use the third person singular of the verb. For example: *¿Tiene usted …?* Do you have …?

Had a go ☐   Nearly there ☐   Nailed it! ☐

Holiday preferences

Preferencias para las vacaciones

1 Lee el texto sobre las preferencias para las vacaciones.

> **Juan:** Yo creo que irse de vacaciones es una idea estupenda, pero preferiría ir después de los exámenes del colegio. Como ya tengo dieciséis años, preferiría pasar las vacaciones con mis amigos en vez de con mis padres, como de costumbre. Así que a partir del diez de junio me vendría bien, porque mi amigo Carlos tiene el último examen el día anterior. Es bastante difícil decidir adónde ir porque somos seis. Todos quieren ir a Grecia, pero yo no estoy tan seguro. Creo que hará demasiado calor.
>
> **María:** No me interesa para nada irme de vacaciones con mis amigos. Dentro de tres meses cumplo dieciocho años, pero no tengo ganas de estar lejos de mi familia, como muchos jóvenes. De hecho, pienso pasar mis vacaciones este año con mis hermanas. La semana que viene vamos a ir juntas a una agencia de viajes para organizar un viaje de tres semanas a México. Es el momento ideal, ya que mi tío está ahora trabajando allí. Si no aprovechamos esta oportunidad será una pena, porque en casa de mi tío no tenemos que pagar alojamiento.

¿Cuáles son las **cuatro** frases correctas?

A	Juan está deseando irse de vacaciones.
B	Juan y María quieren viajar con sus amigos.
C	Juan todavía no ha decidido adónde ir.
D	A Juan le gusta pasar las vacaciones al sol.
E	A María le preocupa lo que va a costar.
F	Juan y María van a celebrar su cumpleaños.
G	María va a reservar sus vacaciones la semana que viene.
H	Juan y María están preocupados por los exámenes.

Escribe la letra correcta en cada casilla.   ☐ ☐ ☐ ☐   **(4 marks)**

Holiday plans

2 You hear two Spanish friends, Chus and Enrique, talking about their holiday plans.

LISTENING
TRACK
59

Listen to the recording

Listen to the recording and write the letter of the correct answer in the boxes.

> This is an example of a longer conversation, where several answers are based on one recording. As you listen for the first time, you can start to eliminate wrong options by putting a little tick, cross or question mark to the right of the options. The second time through, you can complete the process and write the correct letter in the box.

(a) What holiday is Chus recommending?

A	six days in Andalusia
B	a week in Austria
C	a week on the coast

☐   **(1 mark)**

(b) Why does Enrique prefer Cantabria?

A	It's cheaper.
B	It's easier by car.
C	It's a shorter journey.

☐   **(1 mark)**

(c) What does Chus recommend about Ibiza?

A	spending time in the capital
B	the night life
C	sun, sea and sand

☐   **(1 mark)**

(d) What happens in the end?

A	Chus persuades Enrique to go for her idea.
B	Chus accepts Enrique's plan.
C	Chus decides to go on holiday without Enrique.

☐   **(1 mark)**

Holiday destinations

The ideal holiday

1 Read what these young Spanish people say about their ideal holidays.

A	Buscaré la vida nocturna de verano y los centros comerciales, los museos y las galerías. Me gusta el ruido y la actividad. Odiaría una estancia en el campo. **Marta**
B	Ya que mi estación del año favorita es el invierno, iré a un país famoso por la nieve y deportes como el alpinismo y el esquí. La idea de descansar en la playa no me apetece. **Enrique**
C	Iré a países lejanos y distintos para conocer otra cultura, experimentar costumbres nuevas y probar platos picantes. Lo peor para mí serían unas vacaciones deportivas. **Luisa**
D	Una ciudad llena de discotecas y bares no me atrae. Siempre escogeré la tranquilidad de los espacios verdes para andar o ir en bicicleta y escapar del estrés de la vida urbana. **Manuel**

Write the correct letter in each box.

Who …

(a) is not looking for lively night life?   ☐   **(1 mark)**

(b) hopes to travel to faraway places?   ☐   **(1 mark)**

(c) would not like to go on holiday in summer?   ☐   **(1 mark)**

(d) would choose a holiday in the countryside?   ☐   **(1 mark)**

(e) is keen to try foreign food?   ☐   **(1 mark)**

> It is not a good idea to base your answer on one word that you have read. It is essential to take the whole of the texts into account. For example, Marta mentions *vida nocturna* but, in fact, this is something she likes.

Holiday destinations

2 Your Spanish friends have told you about their holiday preferences.

Listen to the recording and complete the sentences in **English**.

Listen to the recording

(a) Carlos wants to go to the ....   **(1 mark)**

(b) Elena prefers to go to the ....   **(1 mark)**

(c) Juan likes going to the ....   **(1 mark)**

(d) Cristina wants to spend time in the ....   **(1 mark)**

(e) Pedro prefers to go to a ....   **(1 mark)**

Travelling

Travel arrangements

1 Read the texts about travel arrangements.

●●○○○ 📶 ▭🔋	●●○○○ 📶 ▭🔋	●●○○○ 📶 ▭🔋
AIDA	**BERNARDO**	**CARMEN**
Llegaré a la estación a las tres. Es el autocar número 6.	Mamá, he perdido el último tren. ¿Podrías venir a buscarme?	Pedro, si compras un billete para Jaén, ¿me compras uno también?
●●○○○ 📶 ▭🔋	●●○○○ 📶 ▭🔋	●●○○○ 📶 ▭🔋
DAVID	**ELENA**	**FRANCISCO**
El tren debería salir en dos minutos, pero va con retraso.	No hay un tren directo. Vamos a tener que cambiar dos veces.	¿Cuánto tiempo dura el viaje? No queremos llegar de noche.

Answer the following questions in **English**. You do not need to write in full sentences.

(a) Where will Aida arrive? .... **(1 mark)**

(b) What does Bernardo need his mum to do? .... **(1 mark)**

(c) What does Carmen ask Pedro to do? .... **(1 mark)**

(d) What is David's problem? .... **(1 mark)**

(e) What will Elena have to do on her journey? .... **(1 mark)**

(f) When does Francisco want to arrive? .... **(1 mark)**

Role play: arranging to visit a friend

> Prepare your answers using the prompts. Then listen to the recording of the teacher's part and answer in the pauses. If you need more time, simply pause the recording.
> An example of a complete role play is recorded in the answer section.

Listen to the recording

2 You are phoning your Spanish friend to confirm the details of your stay with him/her. The teacher will play the part of your friend and will speak first.

You must address your friend as *tú*. You will talk to the teacher using the five prompts below.

Llamas a tu amigo/a para confirmar los detalles de tu visita a su casa.

1 Día y hora de tu llegada

2 Tu viaje – transporte y sitio de llegada

3 !

4 ? Tu llegada a la casa – cómo

5 Idea para una actividad – sábado

> You will find this vocabulary useful:
> luggage – *el equipaje;* suitcase – *la maleta;*
> bag – *la bolsa;* rucksack – *la mochila.*

Holiday activities

On holiday

1 Read what these people say about holidays on a website forum.

A	Me gusta hacer surf y hacer piragüismo.	**Mario**
B	Me encanta nadar y tomar el sol.	**Santiago**
C	Quiero hacer excursiones y comprar recuerdos.	**Felicia**
D	Prefiero visitar pueblos y sacar fotos.	**Daniela**

Write the correct letter in each box.

Who …

(a) likes surfing? ☐ **(1 mark)**

(b) likes to sunbathe? ☐ **(1 mark)**

(c) wants to buy souvenirs? ☐ **(1 mark)**

(d) likes to see the towns? ☐ **(1 mark)**

(e) wants to go canoeing? ☐ **(1 mark)**

(f) likes taking photos? ☐ **(1 mark)**

(g) enjoys a swim? ☐ **(1 mark)**

A typical holiday

2 Listen to Carlos describing a typical holiday.

Write the correct letter in each box.

(a) Who does Carlos normally go on holiday with?

A	girlfriend
B	family
C	friends

☐ **(1 mark)**

(b) Where did he spend the days last year?

A	in the games room
B	on the beach
C	at the pool

☐ **(1 mark)**

(c) What did he do in the afternoons?

A	cycling
B	horse riding
C	fishing

☐ **(1 mark)**

(d) Where did he eat?

A	in the hotel
B	out
C	picnics on the beach

☐ **(1 mark)**

(e) Where did they go if the weather was bad?

A	skating
B	bowling
C	shopping

☐ **(1 mark)**

Listen to the recording

TRACK 62

Holiday experiences

An unforgettable experience

1   Read Guillermo's letter about his holiday.

¡Hola, Ana!

¡Solo volvimos hace dos días, pero ya quiero volver a México! Fueron las mejores dos semanas de mi vida y fue una experiencia maravillosa. Primero fuimos en avión a Nueva York y allí tuvimos que cambiar de aviones. Hubo un retraso de cinco horas debido a lluvias intensas en la Ciudad de México.

Una vez allí, empezó la aventura y viajamos miles de kilómetros en el autocar con los otros viajeros, visitando varias ciudades y sitios de interés histórico. Las ruinas de los aztecas son fascinantes. Los últimos dos días nos alojamos en un hotel en la costa y nos relajamos, tomando el sol y nadando en el mar del Caribe. Una cosa que me sorprendió es que eché de menos la comida española. La mexicana me pareció poco variada.

Un abrazo:

Guillermo

(a) What does the letter tell us?

A	Guillermo returned from holiday two days ago.
B	He was a little disappointed with the holiday overall.
C	They flew directly to Mexico City.
D	Bad weather held up their flight.
E	They stayed in one resort during the fortnight.
F	They travelled with the rest of the tour party.
G	Guillermo found the visits to the ruins a bit boring.
H	For the last two days they were in a seaside resort.

Write the correct letters in the boxes.

☐ ☐ ☐ ☐   **(4 marks)**

(b) What surprised him? ....   **(1 mark)**

(c) What did he think of Mexican food? ....   **(1 mark)**

Holiday memories

2   Listen to Raquel talking about her childhood holidays.

What does she say about the experience?

A	Raquel used to stay with her aunt.
B	The house was in the city.
C	She remembers the sounds and smells.
D	Raquel enjoyed outdoor pursuits.
E	The accommodation was luxurious.
F	Raquel did not go on holiday alone.
G	She stayed there for a few days.
H	She has fond memories of these holidays.

> Note that, in this exercise, Raquel is talking about what she **used to** do when on holiday as a child. The action was recurring, so the verbs are in the imperfect tense. In exercise 1, the action was a one-off holiday in the past, so the preterite is used.

Listen to the recording

Write the correct letters in the boxes.

☐ ☐ ☐ ☐   **(4 marks)**

Transport and directions

Directions to the flat

1 Read Rubén's email giving you directions to his flat.

Answer the following questions in **English**. You do not need to write in full sentences.

¡Hola, David!

El jueves, cuando llegues a la estación, dobla a la derecha al salir y sigue todo recto hasta el río. Cruza el puente y toma la calle San Lorenzo – es la segunda calle a la izquierda. Al final de la calle, llegarás a la Plaza de la Iglesia; tienes que cruzarla y, después, sigue la calle de Correos a la derecha. Toma la tercera calle a la derecha y nuestro bloque de pisos está enfrente de la peluquería.

Hasta pronto.

Rubén

Example: What day will David arrive? Thursday

(a) What should David do first on leaving the station? .... **(1 mark)**

(b) What should he do when he gets to the river? .... **(1 mark)**

(c) Where is San Lorenzo Street? .... **(1 mark)**

(d) What must he cross at the end of the street? .... **(1 mark)**

(e) What building is in the next street? .... **(1 mark)**

(f) Where is the block of flats? .... **(1 mark)**

> You do not need to answer in full sentences. As long as your response makes sense and answers the question, that's all that is necessary. Look at the example: here a one-word answer is enough.

Describing how you travel

2 Tu amigo Ricardo te pregunta sobre cómo viajas.

Escribe una respuesta a Ricardo.

> For the first bullet point you could show off some weather vocabulary instead of repeating the words given. You could start with 'Cuando hace sol …' and 'Cuando llueve …'.

Menciona:

- cómo vas al instituto, con buen tiempo y con mal tiempo

- cómo viajaste cuando fuiste de vacaciones el año pasado

- cómo es el transporte en tu región

- cómo vas a viajar para hacer más ejercicio.

Escribe aproximadamente **90** palabras en **español**.

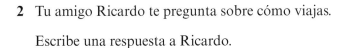

....

....

....

....

....

.... **(16 marks)**

Transport problems

Travel problems

1 Your friend Roberto tells you about a terrible journey.

Answer the following questions in **English**.

Example: For how long did Roberto go to his brother's? *two days*

(a) How was Roberto going to travel to the station? .... **(1 mark)**

(b) What did he have to get first? .... **(1 mark)**

(c) What caused the delays on the road? .... **(1 mark)**

(d) What did Roberto discover at the station? .... **(1 mark)**

(e) What was the problem with the train he got on? .... **(1 mark)**

Role play: reporting an accident

> Prepare your answers using the prompts. Then listen to the recording of the teacher's part and answer in the pauses. If you need more time, simply pause the recording. An example of a complete role play is recorded in the answer section.

2 You are telling the transport police about a road accident that you witnessed. The teacher will play the part of the police officer and will speak first.

You must address the police officer as *usted*. You will talk to the teacher using the five prompts below.

Usted está hablando con un policía sobre un accidente que vio.

    1   Su situación cuando vio el accidente

    2   Qué pasó

    3   !

    4   ? Muchos accidentes allí

    5   Su dirección

> You will need a combination of present, preterite and imperfect tenses: the imperfect to describe where you were and anything that was going on, the preterite for the events that you saw and the present for the first question you ask. Think carefully about which tense you might need to answer the unexpected question.

Holiday problems

Problems in the apartment

1 Señora Martínez is talking to the receptionist.

Listen to the recording and answer the questions in **English**.

Example: What is the number of her apartment? *74*

Listen to the recording

(a) What exactly is the problem with the balcony?

.... **(1 mark)**

(b) What is her second complaint?

.... **(1 mark)**

(c) What is the cause of the problem?

.... **(1 mark)**

(d) What is wrong in the bathroom? Give **two** details.

.... **(2 marks)**

(e) Why does Señora Martínez like the apartment complex? Give **two** details.

.... **(2 marks)**

(f) How would she like to resolve the situation?

.... **(1 mark)**

Translation

2 Translate the following sentences into **Spanish.**

(a) The shower does not work.

.... **(2 marks)**

(b) There are no sheets on the bed.

.... **(2 marks)**

(c) I need two towels in the bathroom.

.... **(2 marks)**

(d) I visited the town yesterday and I lost my passport.

.... **(3 marks)**

(e) The bathroom isn't very clean and the soap is missing.

.... **(3 marks)**

> Because you are dealing with problems, you often need to make negative comments such as 'does **not** work' or 'there are **no** sheets'. Remember to make the verb negative by putting *no* in front: *Hay papel higiénico* = There is toilet paper. *No hay papel higiénico* = There isn't any toilet paper.

Asking for help abroad

Lost property

1 You see this notice in the window of your campsite in Menorca.

Lista de objetos encontrados			
(8 – 15 de agosto)			
Objeto	**Número**	**Objeto**	**Número**
llaves	6	toallas	7
paraguas	4	pendientes	8
gafas de sol	5	móviles	2
relojes	3		

What items are in the lost property office? Complete the sentences in **English**.

Example: There are 7 towels in the office.

(a) There are 4 .... in the office. **(1 mark)**

(b) There are 8 .... in the office. **(1 mark)**

(c) There are 2 .... in the office. **(1 mark)**

(d) There are 6 .... in the office. **(1 mark)**

(e) There are 3 .... in the office. **(1 mark)**

> It is essential to learn vocabulary as you go along, but you can sometimes use word similarities to help you understand. The word *móviles* is only one letter different from its English equivalent and *toallas* is fairly similar to 'towels'. *Paraguas* contains the word *agua*, so it can be linked to 'water' and therefore 'umbrellas'.

Reporting a robbery

2 You hear a woman reporting a robbery in a police station in Alicante.
Listen to the recording and answer the questions in **English.**

Example: What has been stolen? a purse

Listen to the recording

(a) Where was it when it was taken? .... **(1 mark)**

(b) When did it happen? .... **(1 mark)**

(c) How does she describe the stolen item? .... **(1 mark)**

(d) What else might help the police to identify it? .... **(1 mark)**

(e) What must she now do? .... **(1 mark)**

School subjects

Likes and dislikes

1 Read the email from your Spanish friend telling you about his subjects at school.

> ¡Hola! Pronto tengo que decidir las asignaturas que voy a estudiar el año que viene. Sin duda continuaré con el inglés porque es muy útil en el mundo moderno, y también sé que quiero hacer informática. Es una asignatura muy práctica. Mucha gente dice que las ciencias son importantes, pero para mí son aburridísimas. Las matemáticas son una posibilidad porque, para mi sorpresa, las encuentro bastante fáciles. En cambio, es seguro que voy a dejar la historia: es interesante, pero siempre saco malas notas porque es tan difícil aprender todas las fechas.

Answer the following questions in **English**.

Example: What subject does he think is useful? English

(a) Why will he carry on with IT? .... **(1 mark)**

(b) What does he think of science? .... **(1 mark)**

(c) How does he find maths? .... **(1 mark)**

(d) What is his opinion of history? .... **(1 mark)**

(e) Will he carry on with history? Give a reason. .... **(1 mark)**

School subjects

> Prepare your answers using the prompts. Then listen to the recording of the teacher's questions and answer in the pauses. There is a recording of one student's answers in the answer section to give you more ideas.

Listen to the recording

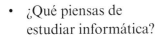

2 Look at the photo and make any notes you wish. You will be asked the following three questions and then **two more questions** which you have not prepared.

- ¿Qué hay en la foto?
- ¿Qué piensas de estudiar informática?
- ¿Qué asignaturas te gustaban en el pasado?

> Note the use of the imperfect tense in the third prompt because you are required to talk about what you **used to** like. Your answer should be in the same tense, for example: *Antes me interesaba … Las clases eran …*

Success in school

How to succeed

Listen to the recording

1 You are attending classes with your Spanish penfriend and listening to the teacher's advice. What is his message?

Write the correct letter in each box.

(a) It's useful to …

A	have a good memory.
B	make a note of everything.
C	record the lessons.

☐ **(1 mark)**

(b) You have to …

A	read through the new work each day.
B	attend all classes.
C	relax at the end of the day.

☐ **(1 mark)**

(c) You need to …

A	report cases of bullying.
B	ask questions as well as answer.
C	avoid interrupting the teacher.

☐ **(1 mark)**

(d) It is advisable to …

A	balance study and leisure.
B	do the hardest homework first.
C	organise your homework diary.

☐ **(1 mark)**

(e) If you miss a lesson, …

A	speak to the teacher next day.
B	email school to let them know.
C	get a study buddy to help.

☐ **(1 mark)**

(f) Success also depends on …

A	a good attendance rate.
B	getting help when you need it.
C	the standard of teaching.

☐ **(1 mark)**

Listen to the recording

Role play: being a better student

> Prepare your answers using the prompts. Then listen to the recording of the teacher's part and answer in the pauses. If you need more time, simply pause the recording. An example of a complete role play is recorded in the answer section.

2 You are talking to your Spanish friend about how to be successful in school. The teacher will play the part of your friend and will speak first.

You must address your friend as *tú*. You will talk to the teacher using the five prompts below.

Estás hablando con tu amigo/a de cómo tener éxito en el instituto.

1   Deberes – recomendación (**un** detalle)

2   Estudiante ideal – conducta en clase (**un** detalle)

3   !

4   Exámenes – preparación (**un** detalle)

5   ? Repaso – cómo

> Question words are used a lot in role plays, so learning them thoroughly will help you. For example, if you are prompted to ask for a reason (*razón*) you will need to ask the question *¿por qué?* (why?). Here, remember that *cómo* means 'how' and can be used in your question.

School life

Parents' evening

1 You accompany your Spanish friend, Alejandro, and his parents to a parents' evening.

What aspects of Alejandro's work is the teacher pleased with?

A	working well in a group
B	involvement in extracurricular activities
C	bringing the right materials to class
D	answering the teacher's questions
E	general progress
F	meeting deadlines
G	remembering his PE kit
H	paying attention in lessons

Write the correct letters in the boxes.

☐ ☐ ☐ ☐

(4 marks)

Role play: talking about school

Prepare your answers using the prompts. Then listen to the recording of the teacher's part and answer in the pauses. If you need more time, simply pause the recording. An example of a complete role play is recorded in the answer section.

2 Your Spanish friend is asking how you are getting on at school. The teacher will play the part of your friend and will speak first.

You must address your friend as *tú*. You will talk to the teacher using the five prompts below.

Estás hablando con tu amigo/a sobre tu instituto.

1 Deberes típicos – tipo (**dos** detalles)

2 Actividades o clubes en el instituto (**dos** detalles)

3 !

4 Uniforme – descripción

5 ? Exámenes recientes –
¿cómo?

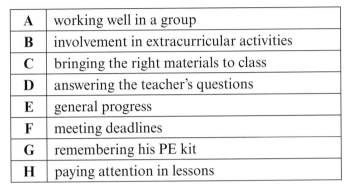

The unprepared question will be in keeping with the rest of the conversation so, during the preparation time, try to think what questions could logically be asked that are on the same topic but are not covered in the other points. You could jot down useful vocabulary as ideas come to you.

The school day

Un día de colegio

1 Lee este correo electrónico de tu amigo mallorquín que describe el día escolar.

> ✉
>
> Las clases empiezan a las ocho, así que durante el invierno todavía es de noche cuando salimos de casa. Vamos en seguida a la primera clase, que ayer fue religión, seguida de física. Después de tres clases tenemos un descanso de media hora, y salimos al patio para charlar y comer un bocadillo que hemos traído de casa. Cada clase dura una hora y el día termina a las dos y media. A esa hora volvemos a casa para comer, y luego por la tarde hacemos los deberes. ¿Cómo es el horario en tu instituto?

Escribe la letra correcta en cada casilla.

(a) Las clases comienzan a las …

A	08:00.
B	08:30.
C	09:00.

A

(d) A media mañana hay un corto …

A	reunión.
B	recreo.
C	examen.

B

(b) Cuando dejan la casa en enero …

A	no hay luz.
B	cogen el autobús.
C	hace frío.

C

(e) A las dos y media …

A	empieza la última clase.
B	van a casa.
C	hacen los deberes.

A

(c) La segunda clase ayer fue …

A	educación física.
B	estudios religiosos.
C	ciencia.

A

(f) El amigo quiere saber …

A	tu opinión de las clases.
B	cómo vas al instituto.
C	los detalles de tu día escolar.

☐

(6 marks)

Mi día en el instituto

2 You phone your Spanish friend Paula to ask about a typical day in her school. Listen to her reply and answer the questions in **English.**

Example: How does Paula go to school? she walks

(a) What time does she leave home? .... **(1 mark)**

(b) Where does she meet her friends? .... **(1 mark)**

(c) How long is break? .... **(1 mark)**

(d) Why don't they have school clubs? .... **(1 mark)**

(e) Give **one** example of what they might do in the afternoon.

.... **(1 mark)**

Comparing schools

A visiting student

1   Pedro, a visiting student, is talking about the differences between your school and his.
    What aspects does he mention?

A	subjects
B	lunch
C	teachers
D	equipment
E	extracurricular activities
F	rules
G	holidays
H	uniform

Write the correct letters in the boxes.

☐ ☐ ☐ ☐   **(4 marks)**

Listen to the recording

Impressions of a British school

2   Read this article from a Spanish school magazine about a student's impressions
    of a British school.

> El centro escolar que visité es un típico instituto mixto de unos mil estudiantes. Lo
> primero que noté fue que solo empiezan a las nueve. En la carretera delante del
> instituto hay atascos y gente impaciente ya que todos los autobuses y los padres en
> sus coches llegan al mismo tiempo. ¡Qué caótico!
>
> A las nueve hay que ir a un aula para que el profe pase lista y luego van a las clases.
> Algunas asignaturas difieren de las nuestras, por ejemplo, se puede estudiar arte
> dramático y empresariales. Durante la hora de comer, sobre las doce y media (¡qué
> temprano!), van al comedor y toman un plato principal y un postre. Después, tienen dos
> horas más de clase antes de terminar el día a las tres y media. Igual que en España,
> tienen deberes cada día, pero aquí suelen hacerlos después de cenar.

Answer the following questions in **English**.

Example: How many pupils go to the school? *about a thousand*

(a) What was the first thing that he noticed? ....   **(1 mark)**

(b) What did he see outside the school? ....   **(1 mark)**

(c) Why did this happen? ....   **(1 mark)**

(d) What started the school day? ....   **(1 mark)**

(e) What **two** subjects would not be studied in Spain? ....   **(2 marks)**

(f) What does he think about the timing of lunch? ....   **(1 mark)**

(g) What similarity does he comment on? ....   **(1 mark)**

> You can sometimes use your cultural knowledge to work out an answer. For question (d),
> you will find in the text that at 9 o'clock they go to a classroom *para que el profe pase
> lista.* You can connect *lista* to the English word 'list', and from your own experience you
> know that first thing in the morning the teacher takes the register, which is a sort of list.

Describing schools

Saber perder **by David Trueba**

1   Read this extract from the text.

> El Instituto Félix Paravicino se fundó en 1932, se amplió en 1967 con un impersonal edificio de hormigón que insulta su original belleza de ladrillo, y en 1985 pasó de femenino a mixto. En el edificio antiguo las escaleras son amplias. En el edificio nuevo las escaleras son estrechas, con reposamanos de pino barato barnizado en brillo. En el edificio viejo las ventanas son grandes, con dos hojas de madera y un cierre de hierro que gira con un roce agradable. En el edificio nuevo las ventanas son de aluminio, con un mango que cruje al accionarse. Los pasillos del viejo edificio son anchos, luminosos, de azulejo modernista. En el nuevo son pasillos angostos, oscuros …

Write the correct letter in each box.

(a)   The school was founded in …

A	1985.
B	1967.
C	1932.

☐

(b)   In the late sixties the school …

A	was extended.
B	received an award.
C	burned down.

☐

(c)   In the eighties …

A	they introduced a uniform.
B	there was a female head teacher.
C	it ceased to be a girls' school.

☐

(d)   The stairs in the new building …

A	lead to the staff room.
B	are too steep.
C	are narrow.

☐

(e)   The new windows …

A	have metal frames.
B	overlook the car park.
C	are large.

☐

(f)   The corridors in the old building …

A	are dark and gloomy.
B	are wide and bright.
C	are long and winding.

☐

(6 marks)

> With challenging reading passages, it helps to have a broad vocabulary in English too. The words *amplió* and *amplias* in the text can both be linked to the English word 'ample', which means 'good-sized' and implies plenty of space. Knowing this can help you to answer two of the questions.

Translation

> In the translation text below there are several adjectives. Your writing in Spanish will be much more accurate if you learn the rules about making adjectives agree.

2   Translate this passage into **Spanish**.

> My school is quite old and has lots of classrooms, three laboratories and a gym. Five years ago they built a big library, which is very modern and has good facilities. Next year they are going to create new tennis courts.

....

....

....

....

(12 marks)

School rules

Las reglas en el nuevo instituto

1 Tu amiga española te muestra las reglas de su nuevo instituto.

Las reglas del instituto

A Hay que llegar a tiempo todos los días y, si algún día llegas después de las ocho, debes presentarte en la oficina de recepción. Si estás ausente algún día, tienes que llevar una carta de los padres al volver a clase.

B Todos los estudiantes tienen el deber de traer todo el material necesario para la clase. También se debe llevar la ropa apropiada.

C No hay que llevar uniforme, pero debes vestirte de una manera limpia y práctica. Las joyas representan un peligro en los laboratorios, así que están prohibidas.

D No debéis llevar artículos de gran valor al instituto como auriculares, móviles y tabletas. Se pierden fácilmente y no los vas a necesitar en clase.

¿En qué regla está la respuesta?

Escribe la letra correcta en cada casilla.

(a) ¿Tengo que comprar uniforme? ☐ **(1 mark)**

(b) ¿Puedo llevar mi ordenador? ☐ **(1 mark)**

(c) ¿Qué hago si llego tarde? ☐ **(1 mark)**

(d) ¿Y si pierdo clases por enfermedad? ☐ **(1 mark)**

(e) ¿Puedo llevar pendientes? ☐ **(1 mark)**

(f) ¿Necesito zapatillas cuando tenemos educación física? ☐ **(1 mark)**

Las reglas de mi instituto

2 Tu amigo/a español/a te ha preguntado sobre las reglas de tu instituto. Escribe un correo electrónico a tu amigo/a. Menciona:

- las reglas de tu instituto y tu opinión

- qué pasó cuando rompiste una de las reglas.

Escribe aproximadamente **150** palabras en **español**. Responde a los dos aspectos de la pregunta. Use una hoja de papel si es necesario.

> Guided

En mi instituto no se puede ....

....

....

....

....

....

....

.... **(32 marks)**

Problems at school

A forum about school

1   Read these entries on an online forum about the problems some students are facing at school.

A	Acabamos de tener exámenes y el viernes pasado descubrí que suspendí casi todos. He perdido todo interés en el colegio y esta semana hice novillos. Es la primera vez que he hecho esto, pero no tengo ningún entusiasmo por ir.
B	No importa cuánto esfuerzo hago, no puedo sacar las notas que mis padres esperan. Paso horas repasando, he dejado de salir con mis amigos y no hago más que estudiar – nada, sólo saco un seis sobre diez.
C	Empiezo a tener miedo de ir al instituto porque una de las chicas mayores me espera en la puerta cada día y me amenaza con golpearme si no le doy dinero. Debería informar a los profesores, pero no sé qué me haría.
D	Todos mis hermanos hicieron ciencias y fueron a la universidad para estudiar medicina, como mi padre, o ingeniería. Detesto esas asignaturas y para mí son dificilísimas. ¿Cómo les puedo decir a mis padres que solo me interesa la cocina?

Who talks about these aspects? Write the correct letter in each box.

(a) Bullying ☐ **(1 mark)**   (e) Family expectations ☐ **(1 mark)**

(b) Studying very hard ☐ **(1 mark)**   (f) Recent exams ☐ **(1 mark)**

(c) Skipping lessons ☐ **(1 mark)**   (g) An unpopular career choice ☐ **(1 mark)**

(d) Lack of social life ☐ **(1 mark)**

> Don't forget that all the texts you read provide opportunities to improve your own speaking and writing by borrowing useful phrases and a variety of ideas to extend your work. You could keep a notebook, divided into topic areas, in which to note down useful vocabulary.

Translation

2   Translate this passage into **English**. Complete the task on a separate piece of paper if necessary.

> Muchos estudiantes dicen que, en la sociedad moderna, hay un alto nivel de presión en los institutos. Piensan que solo es aceptable sacar las mejores notas y estudiar las asignaturas más académicas. Algunos institutos han organizado sesiones después de las clases diseñadas para reducir el estrés que sienten. Estas incluyen la natación, el baloncesto y el monopatinaje.

....

....

....

....

....

....

....   **(9 marks)**

Primary school

At primary school

1 Your Spanish friend tells you what he can remember about primary school.

What does he mention?

A	toys
B	maths
C	teachers
D	history
E	playtime
F	languages
G	dinners
H	uniform

Write the correct letters in the boxes.

☐ ☐ ☐ ☐   **(4 marks)**

Primary school

> Prepare your answers using the prompts. Then listen to the recording of the teacher's questions and answer in the pauses. There is a recording of one student's answers in the answer section to give you more ideas.

2 Look at the photo and make any notes you wish. You will be asked the following three questions and then **two more questions** which you have not prepared.

- ¿Qué hay en la foto?
- ¿Cómo eras de pequeño/a?
- ¿Cómo era tu profesor/a favorito/a?

> Don't be nervous about the imperfect tense, it's actually the most regular tense in Spanish! There are only three irregular verbs:
>
> ser   (era, eras, era, éramos, erais, eran)
>
> ir   (iba, ibas, iba, íbamos, ibais, iban)
>
> ver   (veía, veías, veía, veíamos, veíais, veían)

School trips

Listen to the recording

Our day out

1   Mateo and his friends are talking about their school trips. Where has each person been?

A	bank
B	Roman villa
C	art gallery
D	factory

E	university
F	primary school
G	abroad
H	cinema

Write the correct letter in each box.

(a) Mateo ☐   **(1 mark)**   (c) Alejandro ☐   **(1 mark)**

(b) Carolina ☐   **(1 mark)**   (d) Beatriz ☐   **(1 mark)**

> Listen to the recording twice before you write your answer, to avoid making a mistake that you then have to cross out. As you listen for the first time, you could jot down what you think is the correct letter in the space next to the boxes. The second time round, make your final decision and put the letter in the correct box. In the exam, make sure that you clearly leave just one answer to be marked.

Una excursión con el instituto

2   Tu professor te ha pedido escribir un artículo para la revista escolar sobre una vista que hiciste con el instituto. Escribe el artículo.

Menciona:

- adónde fuiste
- cómo viajaste
- una actividad que hiciste
- tu opinión de la visita y por qué.

Escribe aproximadamente **90** palabras en **español**.

....

....

....

....

....

....

....

....

....

....   **(16 marks)**

School events

The yearly review

1   Read the head teacher's review of events at the school.

> Este año hemos tenido un programa de eventos muy variado. En otoño, el departamento de música organizó un concurso de bandas que fue muy popular con los alumnos de todas las edades. Para Navidad tuvimos un espectáculo de baile, y para celebrar el final del trimestre hubo una fiesta con música de discoteca.
>
> En primavera tuvimos mucho éxito en los deportes, ganando un campeonato de rugby y organizando un torneo de tenis para todos los colegios de la región.
>
> Este trimestre vamos a presentar una obra de teatro y los jóvenes actores están preparándose desde hace siete meses. Sin duda será fenomenal.

Answer the following questions in **English**.

Example: How does he describe the programme of events? *very varied*

(a)   When did the music department organise their event?

.... **(1 mark)**

(b)   What was popular with pupils of all ages?

.... **(1 mark)**

(c)   When was the dance show?

.... **(1 mark)**

(d)   What sporting event did the school win?

.... **(1 mark)**

(e)   How long have the pupils been rehearsing for the play?

.... **(1 mark)**

Topic: School events

> Prepare your answers using the prompts. Then listen to the recording of the teacher's questions and answer in the pauses. There is a recording of one student's answers in the answer section to give you more ideas.

TRACK 78

Listen to the recording

2   Look at the photo and make any notes you wish. You will be asked the following three questions and then **two more questions** which you have not prepared.

- ¿Qué hay en la foto?

- ¿Qué actividades deportivas hay en tu instituto?

- ¿Qué evento te gustaría tener en tu instituto? … ¿Por qué?

> As well as describing exactly what you see (orchestra, instruments) you can also make assumptions based on what you see. For example, here you could suggest that the students have been practising for many months and the teacher is very pleased with them.

School exchanges

The exchange programme

1   Read this programme for your school's Spanish exchange trip.

Answer the following questions in **English**.

Fechas:	marzo 20–27
Transporte:	avión y autocar
Ciudad:	Martorell, a treinta kilómetros de Barcelona
Alojamiento:	con una familia española
Programa:	

· participación en clases
· visita a los monumentos principales de Barcelona
· excursión a la pista de hielo
· cena de despedida en un restaurante

Example: In which month is the exchange? March

(a) How will you be travelling?... **(2 marks)**

(b) Where is Martorell?... **(1 mark)**

(c) Where will you stay?... **(1 mark)**

(d) What will you do in the school?... **(1 mark)**

(e) What sporting activity is planned?... **(1 mark)**

> It is important to know your numbers well, as it is very easy to confuse numbers such as *tres* (three), *trece* (thirteen) and *treinta* (thirty).

Opinions of an exchange

Listen to the recording

2   Your Spanish friend tells you about an exchange visit he went on last year.

(a) Why did he find the visit interesting?

A	He could talk to the students.
B	He learned about the school system.
C	He could ask the teachers questions.
D	He saw which subjects were available.
E	He got some help with his assignment.

Write the correct letters in the boxes.

☐ ☐   **(2 marks)**

(b) Why did he think the exchange was worthwhile?

A	He went out with an English girl.
B	His exam grades improved.
C	He got much better at speaking English.
D	He learned so much about the lifestyle.
E	He attended many cultural events.

Write the correct letters in the boxes.

☐ ☐   **(2 marks)**

(c) What did he have problems with?

A	the food
B	mealtimes
C	going to bed so early
D	finding his way around
E	understanding rapid speech

Write the correct letters in the boxes.

☐ ☐   **(2 marks)**

Future plans

Plans for the future

1 Read these plans on a website forum.

● ● ●

A Cuando deje el instituto, encontraré un trabajo interesante y variado que paguen bien. Los jefes estarán tan impresionados conmigo que me darán varias promociones y después de cinco años viviré en un piso de lujo y tendré un coche deportivo y vacaciones en el Caribe. **Marcos**

B Primero iré a la universidad y cuando termine mi carrera, buscaré trabajo en el extranjero. Con mi experiencia de otras lenguas y culturas conseguiré empleo escribiendo para un periódico y un día todo el mundo me conocerá como presentadora de televisión. **Verónica**

C Soy un chico tradicional de una familia muy feliz y quiero repetir esa experiencia en el futuro. Cuando empiece a ganar un sueldo apropiado, me casaré con mi novia y tendremos hijos. Viviremos en una pequeña casa en las afueras de la ciudad. **Adrián**

D Me casaré con un hombre riquísimo y viajaremos por todo el mundo en su barco. No tendré que hacer las tareas de casa y pasaré el tiempo leyendo revistas, tomando el sol y nadando en la piscina en el jardín. ¡Qué sueño más bonito! **Lucía**

Write the correct letter in each box.

Who …

(a) wants to achieve fame? ☐ **(1 mark)**

(b) will marry for love? ☐ **(1 mark)**

(c) will marry for money? ☐ **(1 mark)**

(d) wants to own expensive things? ☐ **(1 mark)**

(e) plans to lead a lazy lifestyle? ☐ **(1 mark)**

(f) wants an interesting and varied job? ☐ **(1 mark)**

(g) does **not** talk about travel? ☐ **(1 mark)**

> It is important to read all of the texts and not just leap at the first word that matches the question. For example, you might match *vacaciones en el Caribe* (holidays in the Caribbean) with the 'lazy lifestyle' mentioned in question (e), but the rest of the text will lead you to the correct answer.

Las ambiciones de los jóvenes

2 Escuchas un programa de radio sobre las ambiciones de los jóvenes.

Contesta las preguntas en **español.**

Listen to the recording

Ejemplo: ¿Quiénes contestaron la encuesta? *estudiantes de universidad*

(a) ¿Cuántos jóvenes esperaban casarse? .... **(1 mark)**

(b) ¿Cuántos jóvenes querían trabajos motivadores? .... **(1 mark)**

(c) ¿Cuántos jóvenes aspiraban a ser famosos? .... **(1 mark)**

(d) ¿Qué aspecto les importaba a todos? .... **(1 mark)**

(e) ¿Qué quieren tener a los veinticinco años? .... **(1 mark)**

Future education plans

Options at 16

1   Read this extract from a Spanish school's careers guide.

> The text is addressing the students of the school, so it uses the second person plural form of address – 'you' familiar plural.

Al final de este curso vais a terminar la enseñanza secundaria y empezar una nueva fase en la vida. Este es el momento de tomar decisiones para el futuro. Muchos de vosotros vais a continuar con los estudios aquí en el instituto y tenéis que decidir las asignaturas que queréis hacer. Naturalmente, tendréis en cuenta los trabajos que os interesen, pero igualmente importante es que os gusten las asignaturas que escojáis.

Algunos de vosotros seguiréis cursos de formación profesional y hay que investigar bien los cursos disponibles antes de elegir la mejor opción para vuestra personalidad y habilidades.

También existe el mundo del trabajo, pero si preferís seguir esta ruta, es mejor buscar un aprendizaje con una compañía de confianza donde podáis aprender y ganar títulos además de recibir un sueldo.

Write the correct letter in each box.

(a) At the end of the year …

A	they have exams.
B	they go to a new school.
C	they finish secondary school.

☐   **(1 mark)**

(b) If they are staying on, they must …

A	bring a letter of confirmation from home.
B	decide what courses to follow.
C	pass all their subjects this year.

☐   **(1 mark)**

(c) When choosing which subjects to take …

A	enjoyment of the subjects is vital.
B	listen to advice from all sides.
C	pick some new ones for variety.

☐   **(1 mark)**

(d) For vocational courses you should …

A	be aware of the cost of equipment.
B	investigate what the professionals want.
C	look for one that suits you as an individual.

☐   **(1 mark)**

(e) With which type of company should you seek work?

A	reliable
B	local
C	well-known

☐   **(1 mark)**

(f) Why is an apprenticeship recommended?

A	The job prospects are better.
B	You gain qualifications.
C	It's a secure job.

☐   **(1 mark)**

Plans for the future

2   Your exchange partner is talking about her plans for the next few years. What options is she considering?

A	getting an apprenticeship at 18
B	continuing studying
C	getting a degree
D	working in the travel industry
E	taking a year out
F	carrying on with languages
G	looking for part-time work
H	studying sciences

Listen to the recording

Write the correct letters in the boxes.

☐ ☐ ☐ ☐   **(4 marks)**

Using languages

Why study languages?

1 Some Spanish friends are discussing a careers talk they have just attended.

What has each one learned about the benefits of studying languages?

A	English is the language all companies require.
B	You are more employable if you have lived abroad.
C	Languages are essential for work in the tourist industry.
D	You can earn a higher wage.
E	You improve your command of your own language.
F	Companies without linguists lose business.
G	You could get the chance to work abroad.
H	There are more job opportunities.

Write the correct letter in each box.

(a) Álvaro ☐

(b) Nívea ☐

(c) Alejandro ☐

(d) Luz ☐

(4 marks)

Translation

2 Translate this passage into **English.**

> Estudiar español te abrirá muchas puertas a nivel profesional. Hay muchos países que tienen el español como lengua oficial, y por eso hay muchos puestos de trabajo en los que hablar el idioma puede ser un factor fundamental. Saber hablar castellano te ayudará a disfrutar de la literatura y el cine. Es un idioma cada vez más* global e influyente en el mundo de las artes.

....

....

....

....

....

....

....

....

*cada vez más = increasingly/ more and more

(9 marks)

> We use the articles (a/an/the) differently in Spanish and English and you will need to tackle them carefully when translating. The phrase *a nivel profesional* has no article in Spanish but will need an 'a' in English. The phrase *como lengua oficial* is similar.

Jobs

A jobs forum

1 Read these entries on a forum from people who have changed their career path.

● ● ●	
A	Después de ser soldado durante siete años, acabo de empezar la formación para ser bombero. Será un trabajo peligroso pero útil.
B	Me gustaba ser enfermera pero ahora que tengo un hijo no quiero trabajar de noche. Por eso, de momento trabajo como cajera.
C	Estudio para ser farmacéutico y el curso termina este año. Empecé mis estudios con la ambición de ser médico, pero cambié de opinión.
D	Cuando era joven quería ser diseñadora de moda, pero ahora uso mis habilidades creativas en la arquitectura.

Write the correct letter in each box.

Who …

(a) switched degree courses? ☐ **(1 mark)**

(b) is training to be a firefighter? ☐ **(1 mark)**

(c) handles money as part of the job? ☐ **(1 mark)**

(d) has left a military career? ☐ **(1 mark)**

(e) no longer wants to work late hours? ☐ **(1 mark)**

(f) had different aspirations as a child? ☐ **(1 mark)**

(g) has to consider family commitments? ☐ **(1 mark)**

> As well as expressions of time, such as *ahora* (now) and *de momento* (at the moment), it is important to pay attention to the tenses used in order to be clear about when the events are taking place.

La familia de Pablo

2 Tu amigo Pablo te habla de los trabajos de su hermano y su padre.

¿De qué trabajos habla y cuándo?

Completa la tabla en **español**.

Listen to the recording

(a)

En el pasado	Ahora	En el futuro
mecánico		

(2 marks)

(b)

En el pasado	Ahora	En el futuro
	fontanero	

(2 marks)

Opinions about jobs

Opiniones sobre los trabajos

1 Estás escuchando a tu compañero de intercambio que está hablando de unos trabajos posibles.

¿Cuál es su opinión de los trabajos?

A	mal pagado
B	creativo
C	emocionante
D	variado
E	cansador
F	bien pagado
G	aburrido
H	ruidoso

Escribe la letra correcta en cada casilla.

(a) constructor ☐   **(1 mark)**

(b) carpintero ☐   **(1 mark)**

(c) cartero ☐   **(1 mark)**

(d) dependiente ☐   **(1 mark)**

(e) diseñador gráfico ☐   **(1 mark)**

(f) cocinero ☐   **(1 mark)**

> To help you narrow down the options for the answers, listen out for words that are linked to pay.
> Do you hear any of the following: *euros* (euros), *dinero* (money), *ganar* (to earn), *pagar* (to pay), *sueldo* (wage), *salario* (salary)?

Role play: talking about jobs

> Prepare your answers. Then listen to the recording of the teacher's part and answer in the pauses.
> If you need more time, simply pause the recording. The complete role play is recorded in the answer section as an example.

2 You are talking to your exchange partner about possible jobs. The teacher will play the role of your exchange partner and will speak first.

You must address your friend as *tú*. You will talk to the teacher using the five prompts below.

Estás hablando con tu amigo/a sobre trabajos distintos.

     1   Aspectos importantes del trabajo (**dos** detalles)

     2   Tu trabajo menos preferido y **una** razón

     3   **!**

     4   Tu trabajo ideal y **una** razón

     5   **?** Importancia del dinero en el trabajo

> In role plays, you are often required to ask someone for an opinion, so it is a good idea to learn these phrases to start off your question: *¿Piensas que …?*, *¿Crees que …?* (Do you think that …?). A stylish way of asking the same thing is *¿Te parece que …?*

Had a go ☐ **Nearly there** ☐ **Nailed it!** ☐

Applying for jobs

Going for interview

1   Read this extract, adapted from the play *El Método Grönholm* by Jordi Galcerán.

> **ENRIQUE:** Y las condiciones son increíbles. El sueldo es... Bueno, no sé qué debes ganar tú, pero yo casi doblaría... Me preocupaba llegar tarde. Estaba ya en la Castellana, parado, y pensaba, llegarás tarde y quedarás fatal. Estas cosas son importantes. A veces, son los pequeños detalles los que inducen a tomar una decisión. Yo he contratado gente y, al final, lo que me lleva a decidir son los pequeños detalles. La manera de vestir, la forma cómo me han dado la mano... Y el coche. Siempre que puedo los acompaño hasta su coche. Un coche dice mucho de su propietario... Un coche, habla. A veces te encuentras con un tipo que parece muy aseado* y tiene el coche lleno de basura.

*aseado = neat and tidy

Answer the questions in **English**.

(a) If Enrique gets the job, how much will he earn? .... **(1 mark)**

(b) What was making him anxious before he got there? .... **(1 mark)**

(c) Apart from someone's car, what are the **two** other important little details, according to Enrique?

....

.... **(2 marks)**

(d) After interviewing someone, what does he always do if he can?

.... **(1 mark)**

(e) Why does he do this?

.... **(1 mark)**

(f) What has he sometimes found with an apparently neat and tidy person?

.... **(1 mark)**

Translation

2   Traduce el texto siguiente al **español**. Escribe la traducción en una hoja de papel.

> I am creative, hard-working and ambitious and I get on well with other people. I have experience as a waiter in a restaurant and I have worked as a receptionist in a hotel. I speak Spanish and a little French and I understand the importance of good relationships with the customers. The job would be ideal for me.

> Make sure you understand the difference between 'I have' when it means 'I own' or 'I possess' and 'I have' when it is part of a longer verb such as 'I have worked'. The former will be *tengo* and the latter will be *he trabajado*.

....

....

....

.... **(12 marks)**

Careers and training

A letter of enquiry

1　Read the letter below.

> Muy señor mío:
>
> Me dirijo a usted para preguntarle la mejor manera de encontrar trabajo en el campo tecnológico. Me interesa el trabajo de técnico informático porque me gusta la idea de poder resolver los problemas tecnológicos de una compañía y crear soluciones para mejorar sus sistemas. Hasta el momento he estudiado informática hasta el nivel de bachillerato, pero ahora quiero saber la mejor forma de continuar. No sé si quiero seguir estudiando en la universidad, y me gustaría saber si hay cursos de formación más cortos para obtener títulos aceptados en la industria. Sería difícil hacer un internado de varios meses sin ganar nada de dinero, pero ¿piensa que me daría una gran ventaja a la hora de buscar trabajo fijo?
>
> Una última pregunta: ¿Cuál es el mejor sitio para buscar anuncios de trabajo en esta profesión? Espero que pueda ayudarme con estas preguntas y quedo a su disposición.
> Le saluda atentamente
>
> *Arturo Muñoz*

Answer the following questions in **English**.

Example: What is Arturo writing to ask about? how to find work in technology

(a)　What job is Arturo interested in? ....　**(1 mark)**

(b)　Why does he want the job? Give **two** reasons. ....
....　**(2 marks)**

(c)　What qualification does he have? ....　**(1 mark)**

(d)　What alternative to university does he ask about?
....　**(1 mark)**

(e)　Why is he concerned about an internship?
....　**(1 mark)**

(f)　What is his final question?
....　**(1 mark)**

Planning for the future

2　Your Mexican friend, Álvaro, is telling you his plans.

What does he mention?

Listen to the recording

A	gaining work experience
B	his experience of school
C	his chosen profession
D	studying science
E	the subject he wants to specialise in
F	his university friends
G	how much he will earn
H	the length of the training

Write the correct letters in the boxes.

☐　☐　☐　☐　**(4 marks)**

Nouns and articles

Remember not all words ending in *a* are feminine or ending in *o* are masculine! There are exceptions.

1 Write the correct definite article *el, la, los, las*.

Example: la gente

(a) .... mesa

(b) .... fútbol

(c) .... patatas fritas

(d) .... dientes

(e) .... mano

(f) .... piso

(g) .... ciencias

(h) .... guisantes

(i) .... problema

(j) .... foto

2 Complete the sentences with either the definite article *el, la, los, las* or the indefinite article *un, una*. Remember to think about gender and whether it is singular or plural.

Example: En casa tengo un perro que es negro y blanco.

(a) En mi opinión, las zanahorias son más ricas que .... judías verdes.

(b) En mi casa hay .... cuarto de baño y tres dormitorios.

(c) No me gusta nada .... francés porque es complicado.

(d) Todos .... martes tengo club de ajedrez.

(e) En mi estuche hay .... regla y tres bolígrafos.

(f) Mi instituto es grande y hay .... campo de deportes.

(g) Me he roto .... pie y me duele mucho.

(h) .... domingo fuimos a una piscina al aire libre cerca de mi casa.

Often we use articles in English when in Spanish they are not needed, e.g. talking about jobs, and after *sin* and *con*. Sometimes we use articles in Spanish when we would not in English, e.g. talking generally (noun at the start of a sentence), expressing opinions, before the days of the week (*el lunes voy a …*).

3 Read the sentences and cross out any articles that have been used where they are not needed. Note that some sentences may not need to be corrected.

Example: No tengo ~~un~~ coche porque prefiero viajar en metro.

(a) Vivo en un cómodo bloque de pisos en las afueras.

(b) Mi padre es un dentista y mi madre es una enfermera.

(c) Hay muy pocos estudiantes en el instituto sin un móvil.

(d) Escribo con un lápiz en mi clase de matemáticas.

(e) En el futuro me gustaría ser una actriz.

(f) El deporte es muy importante para llevar una vida sana.

(g) Odio el dibujo porque no sé dibujar bien.

(h) Se puede reservar dos habitaciones con una ducha.

Adjectives

Most adjectives agree as follows:

end in *–o*: *alto / alta / altos / altas*

end in *–e*: add *–s* in the plural

end in **consonant***: add *–es* in the plural

*Nationalities also have a separate feminine singular form: *española*

1 Find the correct adjective from the list. Remember that as well as making sense, the adjective must agree with the noun.

Example: una periodista seria

(a) una cama ....

(b) dos gatos ....

(c) un vestido ....

(d) las películas son ....

(e) el profesor es ....

(f) las actrices son ....

(g) la playa es ....

(h) nuestros coches son ....

cómoda
baratos
español
interesantes
preciosa
rojo
~~seria~~
simpáticas
traviesos

2 Choose the correct adjective.

Example: Vivo en un apartamento muy *pequeña /* (*pequeño*) */ pequeños.*

(a) Me alojé en un hotel *lujoso / lujosa / lujosos* de cuatro estrellas.

(b) Me gusta llevar pantalones *cómodas / cómodos / cómodo*.

(c) Creo que mi instituto es bastante *bueno / buen / buena*.

(d) El paisaje era *impresionantes / impresionante / impresionan*.

(e) La estación de tren está siempre *limpia / limpio / limpias*.

(f) Me encantan las ciencias porque son muy *útiles / útil / utilizas*.

Some adjectives have shortened forms which are positioned before the noun:

un coche bueno → *un buen coche*

3 Write out these sentences with the correct adjective in the correct place.

Example: Suelo comer fruta porque es sana y deliciosa. (mucho / mucha)

Suelo comer mucha fruta porque es sana y deliciosa. ....

(a) En Inglaterra hay gente que habla muy bien griego. (poco / poca)

....

(b) Lo mejor es que tiene un jardín. (bonito / bonita)

....

(c) Estamos porque hace buen tiempo. (contento / contentas)

....

(d) En el futuro habrá una estatua aquí en la plaza. (gran / grandes)

....

(e) Nuestro apartamento está en el piso. (primera / primer)

....

Possessives and pronouns

1 Complete the table with the missing possessive adjectives.

English	Spanish singular	Spanish plural
my	mi	
your		tus
his / her / its		
our		nuestros / nuestras
your		
their	su	

2 Complete each sentence with the correct possessive adjective.

(a) My house is big.   .... casa es grande.

(b) His brother is the oldest.   .... hermano es el mayor.

(c) Their sons play tennis.   .... hijos juegan al tenis.

(d) My favourite films are comedies.   .... películas preferidas son las comedias.

(e) Its food is healthy.   .... comida es sana.

Possessive pronouns are like possessive adjectives but replace the noun they describe.
They must agree with the noun they replace!

In Spanish they are always accompanied by the definite article:

el mío / la mía / los míos / las mías = mine	el tuyo / la tuya = yours
el suyo / la suya = his / hers	el nuestro / la nuestra = ours

---

3 Complete these comparisons with the correct possessive pronoun.

Example: Nuestras toallas son más pequeñas que las tuyas (yours)
            (Our towels are smaller than yours.)

(a) Tu perro es más inteligente que .... (mine)

(b) Mis gafas son menos feas que .... (his)

(c) Tu profe de historia es más callado que .... (ours)

(d) Su abrigo es más cómodo que .... (yours)

4 Rewrite the phrases to create one sentence using the relative pronoun *que*.

Example: Tengo un hermano. Se llama Diego. ⟶ Tengo un hermano que se llama Diego.

(a) María tiene un gato. Es negro y pequeño.

....

(b) Vivimos en un pueblo. Está en el norte de Inglaterra.

....

(c) En la clase de literatura tengo que leer un libro. Es muy aburrido.

....

Comparisons

To form the comparative:	*más* + adjective + *que* = more … than
	menos + adjective + *que* = less … than
	tan + adjective + *como* = as … as

1   Read the English and then complete each Spanish sentence with the correct comparative adjective.

     Example: My sister is taller than my brother.

           Mi hermana es ....más alta que.... mi hermano.

     (a) My mother is thinner than my father.

         Mi madre es .... mi padre.

     (b) Mariela is less patient than Francisco.

         Mariela es .... Francisco.

     (c) This bus is slower than the train.

         Este autobús es .... el tren.

     (d) Fruit is as healthy as vegetables.

         La fruta es .... las verduras.

     (e) This shirt is as expensive as that jacket.

         Esta camisa es .... aquella chaqueta.

Remember!

el / la mejor, los / las mejores = the best

el / la peor, los / las peores = the worst

---

2   Write out the correct superlative sentence.

     Example: Esta cafetería es ....la menos cara.... (the least expensive)

     (a) Mi profesor de inglés es .... (the best)

     (b) Mis deberes de religión son .... (the worst)

     (c) Mi mejor amiga es .... de la clase. (the smallest)

     (d) Sus perros son .... (the most intelligent)

     (e) Las noticias de Telecinco son .... (the least boring)

| *el / la* | + | *más* | + | adjective | = the most |
| *los / las* | | *menos* | | | = the least |

3   Translate these sentences into **Spanish**.

To translate words like 'incredibly' or 'extremely' don't forget to use the ending *-ísimo/a*.

     Example: My car is the cheapest. ....Mi coche es el más barato.....

     (a) My cousin is lazier than your uncle. ....

     (b) Her mobile phone is incredibly small. ....

     (c) The Spanish exam is extremely easy. ....

     (d) Horror films are as exciting as action films. ....

     (e) My school is the ugliest! ....

     (f) Science is less boring than geography. ....

     (g) Lionel Messi is the best. ....

Other adjectives

Demonstrative adjectives are used to indicate which thing/person you are referring to ('this', 'those', etc.). There are three in Spanish: one for 'this'/'these', and two for 'that'/'those' (to distinguish between 'that' and 'that further away'). All forms need to agree with their noun in number and gender.

1 Complete the table with the correct demonstrative adjective.

English	Masculine singular	Feminine singular	Masculine plural	Feminine plural
this / these	este			
that / those		esa		
that (over there) / those (over there)			aquellos	

2 Translate into Spanish. (o/t = 'over there')

(a) these boots ....

(b) this T-shirt ....

(c) that girl (o/t) ....

(d) those bananas ....

(e) that mobile phone ....

(f) those magazines (o/t) ....

(g) this book ....

(h) that film ....

(i) that train (o/t) ....

(j) these hats ....

(k) those strawberries ....

(l) those boys (o/t) ....

3 Complete the sentences with the correct indefinite adjectives from the box below.

cada	todo / toda	algún / alguna	otro / otra
mismo / misma	todos / todas	algunos / algunas	otros / otras
mismos / mismas			

(a) Juega al baloncesto ....(every) día.

(b) Siempre da la ....(same) opinión.

(c) Conozco a ....(some) chicas que trabajan como peluqueras.

(d) Ayer, ...(all) los alumnos hicieron sus exámenes.

(e) Voy a hablar con Pablo porque él tiene ....(another) llave.

4 Fill in the gaps in the text using both demonstrative and indefinite adjectives. The text is translated for you below.

El año pasado fui de vacaciones con mi familia. **(a)** ....los años vamos al sur de Inglaterra, pero este año fuimos a España. **(b)** ....de mis amigos han ido a España, pero esta fue mi primera vez. ¡Me gustó mucho! **(c)** ....los españoles que conocimos eran muy amables y **(d)** ....hablaban muy bien inglés. En España, a los jóvenes les gusta la **(e)** ....ropa que a los jóvenes ingleses y nos divierten los **(f)** ....pasatiempos. ¡Fue muy interesante!

Last year I went on holiday with my family. Every year we go to the South of England but this year we went to Spain. Some of my friends have been to Spain but this was my first time. I liked it a lot! All the Spanish people we met were really nice and some spoke very good English. In Spain, the young people love the same clothes as English young people and we like the same hobbies. It was really interesting!

Pronouns

1 Complete the table with the correct subject pronouns in English or Spanish.

yo	
	you singular
	he
ella	

	we (masc.)
nosotras	
vosotros	
	you plural (fem.)
ellos	
	they (fem.)

A pronoun replaces a noun. An object pronoun has the action (shown by the verb) done to it. It can be direct or indirect.

She sent it to me. – **it** = direct object; **me** = indirect object

Direct object pronouns: *me*, *te*, *lo / la*, *nos*, *os*, *los / las*

Position of the object pronouns:

* Before a conjugated verb: *lo compro* (I buy it), *lo he comprado* (I have bought it)

* After a negative: *no lo compro* (I don't buy it)

* At the end of an infinitive or gerund (or before the verb): *voy a comprarlo / lo voy a comprar* (I am going to buy it), *estoy comprándolo / lo estoy comprando* (I am buying it)

2 Replace the noun with the correct object pronoun.

Example: Miguel ha perdido la maleta. ⟶ Miguel la ha perdido.

(a) Hemos perdido las llaves. ....

(b) Han perdido la moto. ....

(c) Teresa come el bocadillo. ....

(d) Compro el vestido. ....

(e) No bebo limonada. ....

(f) No lavo la ropa. ....

(g) Quiero escribir un correo electrónico. ....

(h) No quiero leer esa novela. ....

(i) Necesito la información ahora. ....

(j) Vamos a vender la casa. ....

> Remember!
> You only need to replace the noun. The verb will stay the same.

3 Translate these sentences, which use direct and indirect object pronouns, into English or Spanish.

Example: Le di mi cuaderno de matemáticas. ⟶ I gave him my Maths exercise book.

> Indirect object pronouns: *me*, *te*, *le*, *nos*, *os*, *les*

(a) Le voy a escribir esta tarde. ....

(b) Los visité ayer. ....

(c) Lo haré si tengo tiempo. ....

(d) Le di un regalo para su cumpleaños. ....

(e) ¿Las has visto? ....

(f) She came to visit me at home. ....

(g) They sent me the reservation. ....

(h) I am going to buy them online. ....

The present tense

To form the present tense, replace the infinitive ending with:

–ar verbs: *o, as, a, amos, áis, an*

–er verbs: *o, es, e, emos, éis, en*

–ir verbs: *o, es, e, imos, ís, en*

Tú is used for people you know and in the present tense the verb will always end in *s*.

Usted is the formal word for 'you' and the verb takes the same ending as *él* or *ella*, and therefore has no *s* at the end.

1 Write the verb in the correct person.

Example: escuchar (tú) ⟶ escuchas

(a) vivir (nosotros) ⟶ ....

(b) bailar (ellas) ⟶ ....

(c) vender (yo) ⟶ ....

(d) llevar (vosotros) ⟶ ....

(e) odiar (tú) ⟶ ....

(f) comer (él) ⟶ ....

(g) salir (nosotros) ⟶ ....

(h) escuchar (usted) ⟶ ....

2 Choose the correct verb for each sentence.

Example: En mi tiempo libre *practico* / *practican* deportes.

(a) Mis padres *comemos* / *comen* mucha carne.

(b) Mi hermana y yo *vive* / *vivimos* en un barrio precioso.

(c) ¿A qué hora *tienes* / *tienen* tu clase de natación?

(d) Nunca *habla* / *hablan* en francés porque son tímidos.

(e) Usted *debes* / *debe* firmar aquí.

(f) Nuestro amigo es paciente y nunca *grita* / *gritáis.*

(g) Normalmente *chateas* / *chateo* con mis amigos por Internet.

(h) A veces su profesor *lee* / *leen* en clase.

(i) ¿Usted qué *piensa* / *pensáis* del precio de la gasolina?

(j) *Puedes* / *Podéis* comprar vuestros billetes aquí.

In the present tense, *er* and *ir* verbs are only different for the *nosotros* and *vosotros* parts of the verb and so there are fewer endings to learn!

3 Write the correct part of the verb in each sentence. Watch out for radical-changing verbs!

Example: Mis amigos *estudian* inglés, francés y español. (estudiar)

(a) Nos gusta la comida italiana y esta noche .... pizza. (cenar)

(b) Los mecánicos a veces .... al aire libre. (trabajar)

(c) Me levanto temprano y .... a las ocho y media. (desayunar)

(d) Limpia su dormitorio y luego .... la mesa. (poner)

(e) Nunca comemos caramelos, pero .... pasteles a menudo. (comprar)

(f) ¿Cuánto .... las cebollas? (costar)

(g) .... un cartón de leche, pero no tengo dinero. (querer)

(h) Los niños .... mucho hoy en día. (pedir)

Reflexive verbs (present)

1 Write the correct reflexive pronoun next to each part of the verbs *afeitarse* and *vestirse*.

	afeito			visto
te	afeitas			vistes
	afeita			viste
	afeitamos			vestimos
	afeitáis			vestís
se	afeitan			visten

2 Complete the sentence with the correct reflexive pronoun.

Example: A veces mis amigos no *se* lavan.

(a) Normalmente, los sábados, ………… levanta a las nueve y media.

(b) Mis amigos no ………… peinan, pero yo me peino siempre.

(c) ¿A qué hora ………… despiertas los domingos?

(d) Los profesores ………… quejan mucho de sus alumnos.

(e) Mis primos ………… llaman John y Emma.

(f) ………… levantamos temprano para ir de vacaciones.

(g) ¿………… ducháis por la mañana o por la tarde?

(h) ………… lavas y te vistes antes de ir al colegio.

3 Rewrite the story for Olivia. Change all the verbs in the 'I' form to the 'she' form. Don't forget to change the non-reflexive verbs too!

> Todos los días me levanto temprano para ir a trabajar. Trabajo en una tienda de ropa famosa. Primero me lavo los dientes y luego me ducho y me visto. Bajo las escaleras y desayuno cereales con fruta. Siempre me peino en la cocina. Después, me lavo la cara en el cuarto de baño que está abajo, al lado de la cocina. Me pongo la chaqueta y salgo a las ocho y media porque el autobús llega a las nueve menos cuarto. Vuelvo a casa a las siete de la tarde.

Todos los días Olivia se levanta ....

....

....

....

....

....

....

....

....

....

> Remember! Some verbs are regular but have an irregular ending in the first person singular. *Poner* is one of those verbs: *pongo, pones, pone,* etc. It can be reflexive when it means putting on clothes. Watch out for *salir,* too – the first person is *salgo.*

Irregular verbs (present)

1 Choose the correct verb for each sentence.

Example: Mis padres *decimos* / *dicen* que soy demasiado hablador.

(a) Mi hermano *conduce* / *conduces* como un loco pero yo *conduzco* / *conducen* bien.

(b) Si Pablo *das* / *da* dinero a la causa, yo te *damos* / *doy* una contribución también.

(c) Cuando mi padre *oigo* / *oye* mi música, en seguida *salgo* / *sale* de la habitación.

(d) Si *haces* / *hace* buen tiempo, yo no *coge* / *cojo* el autobús.

(e) Yolanda, cuando tú y Marcos *vienes* / *venís* a casa, siempre *traen* / *traéis* regalos.

2 Complete the sentences with the correct form of the verb.

Example: A las ocho yo ...salgo... (salir) de casa.

(a) Sube el volumen, Carlos no .... (oír) muy bien.

(b) Nunca voy a Francia y, por eso, no .... (conocer) París.

(c) Nuestros primos .... (venir) a cenar esta noche.

(d) Cuando voy a la ciudad siempre .... (coger) el tren.

(e) Cada año, mi familia y yo .... (ir) de vacaciones a España.

(f) Mis amigos han decidido sus asignaturas, pero yo no .... (saber) qué hacer.

(g) Marta, ¿................................. (tener) tu móvil en tu bolso?

(h) Si hace frío en casa, simplemente me .... (poner) un jersey.

(i) Es el cumpleaños de Elena así que yo .... (traer) un pastel.

(j) Mis profesores .... (decir) que voy a sacar buenas notas.

3 Translate these sentences into **Spanish**.

(a) I go to Spain. ....

(b) He has two sisters. ....

(c) I hear music. ....

(d) She tells lies. ....

(e) We catch the bus. ....

(f) They do their homework. ....

(g) You (tú) go out on Saturdays. ....

(h) I give classes. ....

(i) He brings bread. ....

(j) I set the table. ....

> **Vocabulary**
> a lie = *una mentira*
> to set the table = *poner la mesa*

Ser and *estar*

> *ser:* use for permanent things (e.g. nationality, occupation, colour, size, personality)
>
> *estar*: use for temporary things (e.g. illness, appearance, feelings) and location

1 Write the correct form of the verb *ser* or *estar*.

   Example: ..Somos.. ingleses y vivimos en Londres. (ser – nosotros)

   (a) ¿Dónde .... el banco? (estar)

   (b) Mis abuelas .... muy generosas. (ser)

   (c) .... de Madrid, pero trabajo en Barcelona. (ser – yo)

   (d) El vestido .... verde con flores blancas. (ser)

   (e) .... las cuatro y media de la tarde. (ser)

   (f) El armario .... enfrente de la puerta. (estar)

   (g) .... muy tristes hoy porque las vacaciones han terminado. (estar – vosotros)

   (h) .... listos para el examen de teatro. (estar – nosotros)

2 Now translate the sentences from exercise 1 into English. In brackets, write down the reason why
   the verb is *ser* or *estar*.

   Example: We are English and we live in London. ('ser' for nationalities)

   (a) ....

   (b) ....

   (c) ....

   (d) ....

   (e) ....

   (f) ....

   (g) ....

   (h) ....

3 Tick the phrases which use the correct verb 'to be'. Correct those which are wrong.

   Example: Estoy en Francia de vacaciones. ✓

   　　　　　La plaza es a mano izquierda. ✗ La plaza está a mano izquierda.

   (a) Somos británicos y hablamos inglés.

   ....

   (b) Mi amigo está inteligente y tiene el pelo negro.

   ....

   (c) Me duele la cabeza y soy enfermo.

   ....

   (d) Mi perro ha muerto y estoy muy triste.

   ....

   (e) Su primo es italiano y trabaja como diseñador.

   ....

   (f) Mi madre está médica y mi padre está ingeniero.

   ....

   (g) Creo que hoy, después de ir a la peluquería, estoy guapa.

   ....

   (h) Mi casa está bastante pequeña, tiene solo un dormitorio.

   ....

The gerund

Gerunds are *–ing* words (playing, singing, etc.). To form them replace the infinitive endings as follows: *hablar* – *hablando*, *comer* – *comiendo*, *vivir* – *viviendo*.

Remember! Some verbs have irregular gerunds:

caer ⟶ *cayendo*   *oír* ⟶ *oyendo*   *poder* ⟶ *pudiendo*

Some radical-changing *ir* verbs also change their stem in the gerund:

pedir ⟶ *pidiendo*   *dormir* ⟶ *durmiendo*

1 Change the following infinitives into the gerund, and write their meanings in English.

Example: beber ⟶ bebiendo - drinking

(a) comer ⟶ ....

(b) saltar ⟶ ....

(c) correr ⟶ ....

(d) tomar ⟶ ....

(e) dormir ⟶ ....

(f) asistir ⟶ ....

(g) escribir ⟶ ....

(h) escuchar ⟶ ....

(i) aprender ⟶ ....

(j) poder ⟶ ....

2 What are these people doing? Write sentences using the words from the box.

comer pizza	~~nadar en la piscina~~	tocar la guitarra
hablar con amigos	escuchar música	ver una película
navegar por Internet	escribir una postal	montar en bicicleta

Example: (he) Está nadando en la piscina.

(a) (she)...................................
....

(b) (I)...................................
....

(c) (they)...................................
....

(d) (we)...................................
....

(e) (you singular)...............
....

The imperfect continuous is formed using the imperfect tense of *estar* + the gerund:

estaba comiendo – I was eating

estar in the imperfect tense: *estaba, estabas, estaba, estábamos, estabais, estaban*

3 Translate the first part of the sentences into **Spanish**.

Example: (I was fishing) Estaba pescando cuando me caí al agua.

(a) (he was sailing) ....cuando llegó la tormenta.

(b) (they were eating) ....cuando su madre les llamó.

(c) (we were sunbathing) ....cuando empezó a llover.

(d) (you were singing) ....cuando salió el tren.

(e) (we were watching TV) ....cuando nuestro padre volvió a casa.

(f) (I was playing video games) ....cuando llamó.

(g) (you all were listening to the teacher) ....cuando entró el perro.

(h) (she was swimming in the sea) ....cuando apareció el tiburón.

The preterite tense

The preterite tense is used to describe completed actions in the past. Replace the infinitive ending with:

–ar verbs: *é, aste, ó, amos, asteis, aron*

–er and *–ir* verbs: *í, iste, ió, imos, isteis, ieron*

Remember! There are lots of irregular verbs in the preterite.

Some have irregular spellings in the first person: *saqué, toqué, crucé, empecé, llegué, jugué*

The most common irregular verbs are: *ir, ser, hacer, dar, decir, estar* and *tener*.

1 Write the verb in the correct form of the preterite tense.

Example: comer (tú) → *comiste*

(a) sacar (ellos) → ....

(b) volver (nosotros) → ....

(c) comprar (él) → ....

(d) llegar (tú) → ....

(e) trabajar (vosotros) → ....

(f) ir (usted) → ....

(g) dar (yo) → ....

(h) tener (nosotros) → ....

(i) visitar (ellas) → ....

(j) beber (él) → ....

2 Complete the sentences with the verb in the correct form of the preterite. All these sentences use irregular verbs.

(a) La semana pasada .... (ir) a casa de mis amigos.

(b) Mi novio y yo no .... (tener) tiempo para visitar el museo.

(c) Sus padres nos .... (dar) unos regalos bonitos.

(d) Conchita .... (ir) a la playa con su hermano.

(e) El camarero me .... (dar) un café y yo .... (pagar) en seguida.

(f) El invierno pasado mis padres .... (hacer) alpinismo en los Pirineos.

(g) 'No es verdad', ... (decir) el niño.

(h) El concierto .... (ser) impresionante. Me gustó mucho.

(i) .... (hacer) mis deberes antes de jugar al fútbol.

(j) Anoche .... (tener) que poner y quitar la mesa y luego salí con mis amigos.

3 Read the text in the present tense and rewrite it, changing all the verbs in bold into the preterite.

Voy al cine con mis amigos y **vemos** una película de acción. Después **comemos** en un restaurante italiano. **Como** una pizza con jamón y queso, y mi amiga Lola **come** pollo con pasta. **Bebemos** zumo de manzana y mi amigo Tom **come** una tarta de chocolate, pero yo no **como** postre. Después del restaurante **voy** en tren a casa de mi prima. El viaje **es** largo y aburrido. **Vuelvo** a casa y **me acuesto** a las once de la noche.

Fui al cine con mis amigos ....

....

....

....

....

....

....

....

The imperfect tense

Remember! The imperfect is used:
* to describe repeated actions in the past
* when you would say 'used to' in English
* to describe background details.

Replace the infinitive ending with:

–ar verbs: *aba, abas, aba, ábamos, abais, aban*

–er and *–ir* verbs: *ía, ías, ía, íamos, íais, ían*

1   Tick the sentences which contain imperfect verbs and underline the verbs.

   Example: Antes mi colegio <u>era</u> más pequeño. ✓

   (a) El miércoles fuimos a la piscina y nadamos durante una hora y media.

   (b) De pequeños nadábamos en el mar todas las semanas.

   (c) Había mucha gente en el museo y las estatuas eran preciosas.

   (d) Mi padre nos preparó una cena vegetariana.

   (e) Cuando eran más jóvenes, no comían ni tomate ni lechuga.

   (f) Gabriela llegó a Madrid en tren para empezar su nuevo trabajo.

   (g) Ayer nos encontramos en la cafetería y hablamos toda la tarde.

   (h) Me ponía nervioso cada vez que hacía una prueba de vocabulario.

   (i) Lo pasé genial porque hizo sol y no llovió.

   (j) Nevaba todos los días y hacía un frío horrible.

2   Translate the sentences from exercise 1 into English. Explain your choice of tense in brackets. Write your answers on a separate piece of paper.

   Example: My school used to be smaller. (imperfect for 'used to')

3   Complete the sentences with the correct verb in the past tense. It could be either the preterite or the imperfect.

   Example: El sábado ...fuimos... a la discoteca a bailar y a divertirnos. (ir)

   (a) Cuando mi hermana .... tres años empezó a tocar el piano. (tener)

   (b) Mi familia .... en el campo, pero ahora tiene un piso en Londres. (vivir)

   (c) .... mucho calor cuando llegamos al camping. (hacer)

   (d) La semana pasada .... la aspiradora y planché la ropa. (pasar)

   (e) Todos los días .... en el jardín y plantaban muchas rosas. (trabajar)

   (f) Hizo compras por Internet y .... mucho dinero. (gastar)

   (g) Siempre .... fruta y bebíamos mucha agua para estar en forma. (comer)

   (h) Una vez .... al tenis con mi profesor de inglés, pero no gané. (jugar)

The future tense

The **immediate future** tense is used to say what's going to happen. It is formed using the present tense of *ir* + *a* + an infinitive: *Voy a salir a las dos.* I'm going to go out at 2.

Present tense of *ir*: *voy, vas, va, vamos, vais, van*

1   Complete the sentences with the missing parts of the immediate future tense.

Example: I am going to buy a dress.   Voy ª comprar un vestido.

(a) We are going to play basketball.   Vamos a .... al baloncesto.

(b) She is going to lay the table.   .... a poner la mesa.

(c) They are going to eat lamb chops.   Van .... comer chuletas de cordero.

(d) I am not going to cry.   No .... a llorar.

(e) Are you going to watch the film?   ¿............... a ver la película?

(f) You (all) are going to listen and repeat.   .... a escuchar y a repetir.

(g) My mother is going to catch the bus.   Mi madre .... a coger el autobús.

(h) My friends are going to go to Scotland.   Mis amigos van a .... a Escocia.

(i) We are not going to work Saturdays.   No .... a trabajar los sábados.

(j) I am going to go out with my girlfriend.   .... a salir con mi novia.

The **future tense** is used to talk about what you will do or what will happen in the future. The future tense is formed by adding these endings onto the infinitive:

-é, -ás, -á, -emos, -éis, -án

Don't forget the accents!

Remember there are some irregular future verbs: *saldré, diré, tendré, haré, podré, pondré, querré, sabré, vendré.*

2   Write the Spanish for these future sentences. Remember to use the future tense when describing what will happen.

Example: I will buy a dress. Compraré un vestido.

(a) We are going to watch the film. ....

(b) I will not work on Mondays. ....

(c) They are going to catch the underground. ....

(d) He will go to England. ....

(e) They are going to play with my brother. ....

(f) You will go to Spain. ....

3   Complete the text with the correct verbs in the immediate future tense.

seguir	ser	trabajar	tener	ir	tomar	ser	vivir	ir

El año que viene mi amiga **(a)** .... a la universidad a estudiar Biología. Yo no

(b) .... a la universidad porque me **(c)** .... un año sabático. Quiero

trabajar como voluntaria, pero **(d)** .... que vivir con mis padres para ahorrar

dinero. **(e)** .... como voluntaria para una asociación benéfica que cuida a los sin

techo. **(f)** .... muy interesante, pero me imagino que el trabajo

(g) .... muy duro también. Mi hermana **(h)** .... estudiando en el

cole y mi hermano **(i)** .... en el extranjero.

The conditional tense

> The conditional is used to describe what you would do or what would happen in the future. To form the conditional, add the following endings to the infinitive:
>
> *ía, ías, ía, íamos, íais, ían*
>
> There are a few verbs with irregular stems and these are the same as in the future tense.

1   Change these future verbs into the conditional. Write the English for each.

Example: haré ⟶ haría – I would do

(a) compraremos ⟶ ....

(b) saldrán ⟶ ....

(c) trabajaréis ⟶ ....

(d) estará ⟶ ....

(e) jugarás ⟶ ....

(f) vendremos ⟶ ....

(g) podrás ⟶ ....

(h) habrá ⟶ ....

2   In an ideal world, what would happen next year? Create sentences using the conditional.

Example: Mi madre *compraría* un perro.

(a) Mi profesor .... de vacaciones.

(b) Nuestros primos .... el sol en la playa.

(c) El jefe no .... todos los días.

(d) Mis amigos y yo .... la lotería.

(e) No .... contaminación atmosférica.

(f) Más gente .... el transporte público.

(g) Las empresas no .... el agua.

(h) Los gobiernos .... contra la pobreza mundial.

(i) Mi equipo de fútbol .... la liga nacional.

(j) Mi hermano y yo no .... el dormitorio.

malgastar (= to waste)
ir
ganar
haber
compartir
~~comprar~~
trabajar
usar
luchar
tomar
ganar

3   Give advice using the conditional of *deber* or *poder* to help these people.

Example: Tengo dolor de cabeza. –
      Deberías / Podrías tomar una aspirina.

(a) No puedo dormir.

....

(b) Como demasiado chocolate.

....

(c) No tengo energía.

....

tomar una aspirina
acostarte temprano
comer más fruta y verduras
comprar ropa de segunda mano
consumir menos energía
ir al médico
ir al dentista
hacer más ejercicio
evitar el estrés

(d) Estoy enfermo..

(e) Estoy cansado todo el tiempo. ....

(f) Me duelen las muelas. ....

(g) Quiero reducir la contaminación. ....

(h) Debo gastar menos dinero. ....

Perfect and pluperfect

The perfect tense is used to talk about what someone **has done** or what **has happened**; the pluperfect is used to talk about what someone **had done** or what **had happened**.

Perfect: present tense of *haber* + a past participle.

Pluperfect: imperfect tense of *haber* + a past participle.

To form the past participle replace the infinitive ending with:
–ar verbs: *ado*
–er and *–ir* verbs: *ido*

1   Complete the table with the correct parts of the verb *haber*.

	Perfect tense (I have … etc.)	Pluperfect tense (I had … etc.)	+ past participles (spoken, eaten, lived, etc.)
yo	he		hablado comido vivido
tú			hablado comido vivido
él / ella / usted		había	hablado comido vivido
nosotros / nosotras	hemos		hablado comido vivido
vosotros /vosotras			hablado comido vivido
ellos / ellas / ustedes		habían	hablado comido vivido

Irregular past participles!

abrir → abierto	escribir → escrito	poner → puesto	ver → visto
decir → dicho	hacer → hecho	romper → roto	volver → vuelto

2   Translate these phrases into English or Spanish. The box above will help you.

Example: He hablado con él. I have spoken to him.

(a)   Hemos perdido el tren. ....

(b)   ¿Has estudiado español? ....

(c)   Han comprado un ordenador portátil. ....

(d)   He hecho los deberes. ....

(e)   Hemos visto un documental muy informativo. ....

(f)   I have broken my arm. ....

(g)   They have lost their suitcase. ....

(h)   We have eaten lots of sweets. ....

(i)   Have you visited the museum today? ....

(j)   The air stewards have opened the doors. ....

3   Change the verbs into the pluperfect to tell the story.

Esta mañana ha sido horrible. **(a)** Yo ya había desayunado (desayunar) cuando sonó mi móvil. Mi amiga **(b)** .... (perder) el bolso en el polideportivo y no tenía dinero suficiente para volver a su casa. Ella **(c)** .... (nadar) en la piscina y también **(d)** .... (ir) a una clase de aerobic. Así que fui al polideportivo para ayudarla, pero yo me **(e)** .... (dejar) la bici en el cole y por eso cogí el autobús. El viaje duró mucho y cuando llegué, mi amiga ya **(f)** .... (encontrar) su bolso y su dinero. ¡Qué desastre!

Giving instructions

To give commands:

– to one person (**tú**): use the 'you' singular form of the present tense, minus the final *s*:
¡Escucha! Listen!   *¡Abre!* Open!

– to more than one person (**vosotros**): change the final *r* of the infinitive to *d*:
¡Escuchad! Listen!   *¡Abrid!* Open!

Irregular *tú* commands include:

	decir	hacer	ir	oír	poner	salir	tener	venir
tú	di	haz	ve	oye	pon	sal	ten	ven
English	say	make/do	go	hear	put	leave	have	come

1 Change the following infinitives into familiar singular commands (*tú*). Be careful, some are irregular in the command form.

   Example: Hablar más ⟶ Habla más.

   (a) Doblar a la derecha ⟶ ....   (f) Cantar más bajo ⟶ ....

   (b) Cruzar la plaza ⟶ ....   (g) Leer en voz alta ⟶ ....

   (c) Pasar el puente ⟶ ....   (h) Escuchar bien ⟶ ....

   (d) Tener cuidado ⟶ ....   (i) Poner la mesa ⟶ ....

   (e) Venir aquí ⟶ ....   (j) Hacer este ejercicio ⟶ ....

2 Now change the above commands into familiar plural ones (*vosotros*). Remember, to form the *vosotros* commands, you change the *r* of the infinitive to *d*.

   Example: Habla más. ⟶ Hablad más.

   (a) ....   (f) ....

   (b) ....   (g) ....

   (c) ....   (h) ....

   (d) ....   (i) ....

   (e) ....   (j) ....

3 Translate these sentences into **Spanish**, using either *tú* or *vosotros* commands.

   Example: Listen now! (vosotros) ⟶ ¡Escuchad ahora!

   (a) Download the music! (tú) ....

   (b) Turn left! (vosotros) ....

   (c) Clear the table! (tú) ....

   (d) Make the bed! (tú) ....

   (e) Do the vacuuming! (vosotros) ....

The present subjunctive

The subjunctive is used in a range of contexts, e.g.

– to express doubt or uncertainty: *No creo que venga.* I don't think he's coming.

– to express a wish with **querer que**: *Quiero que te calles.* I wish you'd be quiet.

– after **cuando** with the future: *Cuando llegue, le contestaré.* When he arrives, I'll ask him.

– after **ojalá**: *Ojalá haga sol.* Let's hope it's sunny.

– to deny that information is true: *No es verdad que sea tímida.* It's not true that she's shy.

– to give negative *tú* commands: *¡No vayas!* Don't go!

The subjunctive is formed by replacing the *–o* ending of the present tense 'I' form with:

–ar verbs: *e, es, e, emos, éis, en*

–er and *–ir* verbs: *a, as, a, amos, áis, an*

Therefore verbs which are irregular in the first person in the present are irregular in the present subjunctive.

ir and *ser* have irregular stems: *vay– (ir)* and *se– (ser)*. The endings are the same.

1   Change these verbs from the present indicative into the present subjunctive.

Example: tenemos → tengamos

(a) habla → ....
(b) comen → ....
(c) voy → ....
(d) vives → ....
(e) trabajáis → ....
(f) sale → ....
(g) puede → ....
(h) hacen → ....
(i) encuentro → ....
(j) somos → ....

2   Use the present subjunctive to make these positive *tú* commands into negative ones.

Example: Habla con él. → No hables con él.

(a) Come este pastel. → ....
(b) Compra aquel vestido. → ....
(c) Toma esa calle. → ....
(d) Bebe un vaso de zumo de naranja. → ....
(e) Ved esta película romántica. → ....
(f) Firmad aquí. → ....
(g) Rellenad este formulario. → ....
(h) Abrid las ventanas. → ....

3   Complete these sentences with the verb in the correct form of the present subjunctive.

Example: Ojalá mi amiga venga (venir) a visitarme.

(a) No creo que los jóvenes .... (trabajar) tanto.
(b) No es cierto que .... (hacer) siempre calor en el sur.
(c) Ojalá nosotros .... (tener) suerte con los exámenes.
(d) No creo que mis profesores .... (ser) estrictos.
(e) Cuando .... (ir) a España, compraré un sombrero.
(f) Dudo que los adolescentes .... (comprar) esos CD.

Negatives

> To make a sentence negative, use *no* in front of the whole verb:
>
> | | |
> |---|---|
> | *No me gusta la música jazz.* | I don't like jazz music. |
> | *No vamos a visitar el palacio.* | We are not going to visit the palace. |

1   Write these sentences in the negative.

Example: Tengo clase hoy a las diez. ⟶ No tengo clase hoy a las diez.

(a) Estudio geografía. ⟶ ....

(b) Vamos a las afueras. ⟶ ....

(c) Ricardo compró una moto nueva. ⟶ ....

(d) Sus padres vieron la tele. ⟶ ....

(e) Voy a ir a Francia la semana que viene. ⟶ ....

2   Match the English and Spanish.

1	no … ni … ni …	**A**	never
2	no … nada	**B**	not … either
3	no … tampoco	**C**	no/not any
4	no … nadie	**D**	nothing/not anything
5	no … jamás	**E**	not … (either) … or …
6	no … nunca	**F**	never
7	no … ningún/ninguna	**G**	no one

3   Rewrite the sentence in the negative form using the words in brackets.

Example: Mateo habla mucho de sus vacaciones. (no, nunca)
Mateo no habla nunca de sus vacaciones.

> Note that *ninguno* must agree with the noun it precedes: *ninguna ropa* (no clothes)

(a) Mis profesores enseñan cómo repasar. (no, nunca) ....

(b) En mi casa tuvimos una sala de juegos. (no, jamás) ....

(c) Me he quemado los brazos. (no, nunca) ....

(d) Aquí tengo vestidos, faldas y camisetas. (no, ni, ni, ni) ....

(e) Vas a comprar un coche. (no, ningún) ....

(f) Mis padres escuchan. (no, a nadie) ....

4   Translate the sentences into **Spanish**. Be careful with the word order.

Example: He never plays football when it rains.
Nunca juega al fútbol cuando llueve. / No juega nunca al fútbol cuando llueve.

(a) In the afternoon we never drink coffee. ....

(b) I don't iron, cook or clean. ....

(c) They do not speak any languages. ....

(d) We can't talk to anybody during the exam. ....

....

(e) I will never smoke because it is a waste of money. ....

....

Special verbs

A few verbs like *gustar* are generally used in the 3rd person with a pronoun:
Me gusta bailar. I like dancing.

If the thing that is liked is plural, you use *me gustan*: *Me gustan los perros.* I like dogs.
encantar, *doler*, *apetecer* and *faltar* behave in the same way:
Le duele la cabeza. His head hurts.
Hacen falta dos vasos. Two glasses are needed.
¿Te apetece salir a comer? Do you fancy going out to eat?

1 Complete the table with the correct pronouns.

me	gusta (sing)	I like
		you like
	gustan (pl)	he / she / it likes

	gusta (sing)	we like
		you (all) like
	gustan (pl)	they like

2 Tick the sentences which use the impersonal verb correctly. Correct the other sentences.

Remember! If the impersonal verb is followed by an infinitive, the singular form is always used:
*Les **gusta** tocar la guitarra.* = They like to play the guitar.
When the subject is a noun or a proper noun, you need to use *a*:
A Paz le gusta correr. = Paz likes to run.

Example: Me gusta mucho los idiomas y por eso quiero viajar más. ✗
Me gustan mucho los idiomas y por eso quiero viajar más.

(a) A Pilar y a Pablo les interesan los ordenadores y la informática.

....

(b) Nos apetecen ir al teatro mañana.

....

(c) Es verdad que le duelen mucho los ojos.

....

(d) No nos gustan la contaminación atmosférica.

....

(e) ¿Te hace falta unas toallas?

....

3 Unjumble the words to make sentences using an impersonal verb.
Example: gustan / las / me / zanahorias / mucho Me gustan mucho las zanahorias.
(a) falta / abrigo / nos / un / hace ....
(b) os / caballos / encantan / los / negros ....
(c) María / le / aquellos / zapatos / a / gustan ....
(d) quedan / veinte / te / euros / regalo / comprar / para / el

....

(e) todo / me / el / la / cabeza / tiempo / duele

....

(f) encantan / rascacielos / porque / les / son / modernos / los

....

Had a go ☐   **Nearly there** ☐   **Nailed it!** ☐

Por and *para*

> Remember that *por* and *para* don't just mean 'for'. They can be translated in various ways depending on the sentence. For example: in, in order to, per, instead of, etc.

1 Translate these sentences, which use *para*, into **English**.

(a) Para mi cumpleaños quiero un móvil nuevo.

....

(b) Mi amiga trabaja para un arquitecto.

....

(c) Las aplicaciones para iPhone son increíbles.

....

(d) Como muchas verduras y pescado para estar en forma.

....

(e) Necesitas la llave para entrar en casa.

....

(f) Fumar es muy malo para la salud.

....

(g) Van a organizar una fiesta para celebrar el fin de curso.

....

(h) Para mí, los deportes son siempre divertidos.

....

2 Rewrite the sentences with the word *por* in the correct place.

Example: Muchas gracias los pantalones. Muchas gracias por los pantalones.

(a) El coche rojo pasó las calles antiguas.

....

(b) Normalmente la mañana me gusta desayunar cereales y fruta.

....

(c) Mandé la reserva correo electrónico.

....

(d) Me gustaría cambiar este jersey otro.

....

(e) En la tienda ganamos diez euros hora.

....

(f) Había mucha basura todas partes.

....

3 Complete the sentence with either *por* or *para*.

Example: ...Por... la tarde prefiero descansar.

(a) .... perder peso, lo más importante es beber mucha agua.

(b) Mis amigas compraron unas flores .... la profesora.

(c) Tengo que cambiar este diccionario .... otro.

(d) Hemos reservado una habitación .... tres noches.

(e) Los alumnos tienen que completar los ejercicios .... el lunes.

Questions and exclamations

Don't forget that Spanish question words have accents. Questions and exclamations have an inverted question mark (¿) or exclamation mark (¡) at the beginning.

1 Use the question words in the box to complete the table below.

¿Qué?	¿Cuánto?	¿Dónde?	¿Cuándo?	¿Cuáles?
¿Adónde?	¿Por qué?	¿Cuántos?	¿Cómo?	¿Cuál?

Why?	
What?	¿Qué?
When?	
How?	
Where?	
Where to?	
Which?	¿Cuál?
Which ones?	
How much?	
How many?	

2 Match the Spanish and the English for these exclamations. Write the correct letters in the grid.

1 ¡Qué lástima!		**A** What a problem!
2 ¡Qué va!		**B** How strange!
3 ¡Qué rollo!		**C** How cool!
4 ¡Qué difícil!		**D** How terrible!
5 ¡Qué problema!		**E** No way!
6 ¡Qué guay!		**F** What a shame!
7 ¡Qué bien!		**G** How boring!
8 ¡Qué raro!		**H** How embarrassing!
9 ¡Qué vergüenza!		**I** How good!
10 ¡Qué horror!		**J** How difficult!

1	2	3	4	5	6	7	8	9	10
F									

3 Complete the question or exclamation with the appropriate word or phrase.

rollo	guay	cómo	cuánto	dónde	horror

Example: ¿De _dónde_ son ustedes?

(a) Me he roto la pierna. ¡Qué .... !

(b) ¿ .... cuesta el jamón serrano?

(c) ¿ .... es tu casa, Ramona?

(d) Vamos a ir de vacaciones.

    ¡Qué .... !

(e) El viaje en autocar va a durar ocho horas.

    ¡Qué .... !

Connectives and adverbs

Not all adverbs end in *–mente*:

bien – well   *siempre* – always   *bastante* – enough   *poco* – a little
mal – badly   *demasiado* – too   *a menudo* – frequently / often

1 Turn these adjectives into adverbs. Remember to make them feminine first!

Example: fácil → fácilmente

(a) rápido → ....

(d) alegre → ....

(b) difícil → ....

(e) tranquilo → ....

(c) lento → ....

2 Match the connectives correctly. Write the correct letters in the grid.

1 además de	**A** but
2 y / e	**B** therefore
3 pero	**C** although
4 sin embargo	**D** also
5 también	**E** and
6 por eso / por lo tanto	**F** if
7 porque	**G** because
8 ya que	**H** then
9 si	**I** or
10 o / u	**J** since
11 aunque	**K** however
12 entonces	**L** as well as

1	2	3	4	5	6	7	8	9	10	11	12
L											

3 Rewrite sentences a–e with the correct adverb. Complete sentences f–h with the correct connective.

Example: Los alumnos juegan al rugby. (well) Los alumnos juegan bien al rugby.

(a) Sus padres cantan en la iglesia. (badly)

....

(b) No hablo porque soy tímido. (much)

....

(c) El tren pasa por el túnel. (quickly)

....

(d) Los pendientes son caros. (too)

....

(e) Comemos huevos por la mañana. (frequently)

....

(f) Vamos a ir a la piscina .... hace buen tiempo.

(g) Odio mi instituto .... hay acoso escolar.

(h) El piso es muy moderno, ... no tiene lavaplatos.

Remember! Adverbs can go before or after the verb they relate to:
Siempre como carne. / Como siempre carne.

Numbers

1 Write the number.

Example: trece 13

(a) veinte ....

(b) cuarenta y ocho ....

(c) nueve ....

(d) cien ....

(e) catorce ....

(f) mil ....

(g) trescientos ....

(h) cincuenta y siete ....

(i) veintitrés ....

(j) quince ....

(k) diecinueve ....

(l) quinientos ....

(m) un millón ....

(n) novecientos ....

(o) ochenta y ocho ....

(p) setenta y seis ....

(q) sesenta y siete ....

(r) diez ....

(s) cero ....

(t) veintinueve ....

> Ordinal numbers (*primero*, *segundo*, *tercero*, etc.) are not used for dates, except for *primero* which can be used. Both of these are correct:
>
> *el uno de diciembre*
>
> *el primero de diciembre*

2 Write these dates and years in **Spanish**.

Example: 4 May *el cuatro de mayo*

(a) 1999 ....

(b) 10 October ....

(c) 1 January ....

(d) 3 March ....

(e) 2013 ....

(f) 16 November ....

(g) 30 May ....

(h) 1968 ....

(i) 2002 ....

(j) 21 April ....

> To give the time, use *son las* + the number for the hour, except for 'one o'clock', which is *Es la una*.
> *Son las ocho.* It's eight o'clock.
> For times **past** the hour, add *y cinco, y diez* etc.: *Son las nueve y veinte.*
> For times **to** the hour, add *menos veinte, menos diez* etc.: *Son las tres menos diez.*
> a quarter past = *y cuarto*
> a quarter to = *menos cuarto*
> half past = *y media*

3 Write these times in **Spanish**.

Example: It's 5.25. *Son las cinco y veinticinco*

(a) It's 7.15 ....

(b) It's 1.25 ....

(c) It's 8.35. ....

(d) It's 11.10. ....

(e) It's 3.45. ....

(f) It's 9.50. ....

(g) It's 5.30. ....

(h) It's 12.00. ....

Practice test: Listening 1

Food and drink

Listen to the recording

1 Listen to Sergio talk about what he usually eats.

What does he say? Answer the questions in **English**.

Example: What does Sergio have for breakfast? *cereal*

(a) What does he have at break? .... **(1 mark)**

(b) What is his favourite meal at lunch? .... **(1 mark)**

(c) What do they often have as a main course in the evening?

.... **(1 mark)**

Holidays

Listen to the recording

2 Your Spanish exchange partner, Verónica, is telling you about her trip to México.

What holiday highlights does she mention?

A	visiting ancient monuments
B	watching a dance show
C	being serenaded
D	shopping for souvenirs
E	sampling the traditional food
F	seeing famous paintings
G	sunbathing on the beach
H	taking a boat trip

Write the correct letters in the boxes.

A ☐ ☐ ☐   **(3 marks)**

Practice test: Listening 2

School activities

Listen to the recording

1 Your Spanish friends are telling you about the school activities they are involved in.

A	extra language lessons
B	chess club
C	plays and shows
D	working in the school snack bar
E	training with the athletics team
F	singing in the choir

What does each person do?

Write the correct letter in each box.

Example: Alba   A

(a) Rubén   ☐

(b) Teresa   ☐

(c) Álvaro   ☐   **(3 marks)**

Directions

Listen to the recording

2 You are listening to your Spanish friend's voicemail giving you directions to her house.

Complete the sentences. Write the correct letter in each box.

A	next to
B	station
C	square
D	bridge
E	right
F	church
G	opposite
H	left
I	straight on
J	park

(a) When you leave the B you need to turn ☐ .

(b) At the crossroads, go ☐ and then cross the ☐ .

(c) When you get to the ☐ , you're nearly there: my house is ☐ the petrol station.

(5 marks)

Practice test: Listening 3

Weather report

1 You are listening to the weather forecast in northern Spain trying to plan your week.

What sort of weather are you going to have?

A	hot
B	snow
C	wind
D	storms
E	rain
F	fog
G	hail
H	cold

Write the correct letters in the boxes.

[D] ☐ ☐ ☐

(3 marks)

Problems with a hotel

2 You hear Señor Castillo talking to the receptionist in your hotel.

Write the correct letter in each box.

(a) What does Señor Castillo want to do?

A	book a room
B	change rooms
C	check in

☐

(b) Which of these does he **not** want?

A	a balcony
B	the evening meal
C	to overlook the street

☐

(c) What room does the receptionist offer?

A	one with a double bed and a balcony
B	one with single beds and a balcony
C	one with single beds and no balcony

☐

(d) What does the room overlook?

A	the grounds
B	the lake
C	the pool

☐

(e) What does she say about the room?

A	It is smaller than the others.
B	It is available in an hour.
C	It costs a little bit more.

☐

(f) Why does Señor Castillo take the room?

A	He will get a good view of the festival.
B	It will be a lot quieter.
C	The couple in the next room are not noisy.

☐

(6 marks)

Practice test: Speaking 1

Topic: At the tourist office

1 Instructions to candidates:

Your teacher will play the role of an employee at the tourist office and will speak first.

You should address the assistant as *usted*.

When you see this – **!** – you will have to respond to something you have not prepared.

When you see this – **?** – you will have to ask a question.

> Spend about 12 minutes preparing the following role play, using the prompts below. Then listen to the teacher's part and answer in the pauses. Finally, listen to the sample answers in the answers section.

> Usted está hablando con el empleado / la empleada de una oficina de turismo en Andalucía (España).
>
> 1   Sitios de interés – información
>
> 2   Región – mapa
>
> 3   **!**
>
> 4   Estancia en la ciudad – duración
>
> 5   **?** Excursiones – barco

Topic: Hobbies and free time

2 Instructions to candidates:

Your teacher will play the role of your Spanish friend and will speak first.

You should address your friend as *tú*.

When you see this – **!** – you will have to respond to something you have not prepared.

When you see this – **?** – you will have to ask a question.

> Spend about 12 minutes preparing the following role play, using the prompts below. Then listen to the teacher's part and answer in the pauses. Finally, listen to the sample answers in the answers section.

> Estás hablando con tu amigo/a español/a sobre tu tiempo libre.
>
> 1   Actividades en la casa (**dos** detalles)
>
> 2   Actividades con amigos (**dos** detalles)
>
> 3   **!**
>
> 4   Pasatiempo futuro
>
> 5   **?** Deberes – cantidad

Practice test: Speaking 2

Life at school

1 Candidate's photo card

- Look at the photo during the preparation period.

- Make any notes you wish to on an Additional Answer Sheet.

- Your teacher will then ask you questions about the photo and about topics related to **life at school**.

Your teacher will ask you the following three questions and then **two more questions** which you have not prepared.

- ¿Qué hay en la foto?

- ¿Cuál es tu asignatura favorita y por qué?

- ¿Qué hiciste en tu última clase de español?

> Spend about 12 minutes preparing the following photo-based task, using the prompts below. Then listen to the teacher's part and answer in the pauses. Finally listen to the sample answers in the answers section.

2 Candidate's photo card

- Look at the photo during the preparation period.

- Make any notes you wish to on an Additional Answer Sheet.

- Your teacher will then ask you questions about the photo and about topics related to **life at school**.

Your teacher will ask you the following three questions and then **two more questions** which you have not prepared.

- ¿Qué hay en la foto?

- ¿Cuáles son las presiones de los estudios?

- ¿Qué te gustaría cambiar de tu instituto y por qué?

Practice test: Reading 1

Social media and technology

1 Read these entries on a Spanish website about the best aspects of technology.

Lorena	Lo mejor es la cantidad de información a la que puedes acceder. Si tienes una pregunta, no tienes que pasar tiempo tratando de recordar la respuesta, solo haces clic y la red te da lo que buscas.
Alejandro	Para mí lo mejor es poder estar conectado a todas horas. Si usas correos electrónicos o mensajes en una red social puedes comunicarte en un momento con amigos que están cerca o con familiares al otro lado del mundo.
Paula	El mejor aspecto para mí es la capacidad de crear obras de arte. Yo uso aplicaciones de diseño y es increíble lo que puedes producir con un nivel casi profesional. Espero trabajar en diseño cuando termine mis estudios.
David	En mi opinión, lo más impresionante es la transformación en la manera en que escuchamos canciones. Es tan fácil descargarlas al móvil o al ordenador y, en muchas ocasiones, también es muy barato.

Which statement matches which person? Write the correct letter in each box.

A	I am developing skills for a future career.
B	I use it to research trips abroad and hotel prices.
C	I love the way the internet answers questions in seconds.
D	I use it to listen to music.
E	I use it to do research for art homework.
F	I like to keep in touch with people abroad.
G	I create work sheets and revision packs for my students.

(a) Lorena ☐   (c) Paula ☐

(b) Alejandro ☐   (d) David ☐   **(4 marks)**

Translation

2 You have received this post on Facebook. Translate it into **English** for your friend.

> Si quiero comprar ropa, voy a la ciudad en tren o en autobús y mis amigos y yo vamos al centro comercial. El sábado pasado compré un regalo para mi madre porque es su cumpleaños mañana. Iré a la tienda con mi padre para escoger una tarta.

....

....

....

....

....

.... **(9 marks)**

Practice test: Reading 2

Festivals

1   Read this article on a Spanish travel website about the Lanzada beach in Galicia.

> ✉
>
> En Galicia existe una vieja tradición que tiene lugar cada año, el último domingo de agosto. Durante el resto de la temporada la playa de Lanzada está llena de niños que juegan mientras sus padres descansan. Sin embargo, ese domingo es especial porque las mujeres casadas que quieren tener un hijo vienen a bañarse en el mar. Es un rito de fertilidad. Según la leyenda, si la mujer se queda en el mar hasta que pasen nueve olas,* tendrá un hijo el siguiente año.

*ola = wave

Answer the following questions in **English**.

(a) When does the tradition take place?

.... **(1 mark)**

(b) What happens on the beach the rest of the year?

.... **(1 mark)**

(c) Who takes part in the event?

.... **(1 mark)**

(d) What must they do to make their wish come true?

.... **(1 mark)**

(e) What will then happen?

.... **(1 mark)**

Back to school

2   Read this extract from a letter from your Spanish friend.

> El profesor empezó por recordarnos las reglas del instituto (algunas tontas, algunas razonables) y luego nos dio el horario. Resulta que tengo física el viernes por la tarde, ¡qué horror! Quería dejarla, pero hay que estudiarla si quieres hacer ingeniería en el futuro. Tengo una clase de inglés a primera hora el lunes. No es el mejor momento para hablar un idioma extranjero. Es muy temprano y todavía tienes sueño.

Write the correct letter in each box.

Example: The first thing they discussed was…

A	materials to bring to class.
B	**school rules.**
C	the timetable.

B

(a) Regarding the rules, your friend has…

A	a negative opinion.
B	found them very sensible.
C	mixed views.

☐

(b) He comments that physics …

A	is not on his timetable.
B	is his favourite subject.
C	is his last lesson of the week.

☐

(c) The English lesson …

A	always sends him to sleep.
B	is not scheduled at the ideal time.
C	is first thing on Tuesday.

☐

(3 marks)

Practice test: Reading 3

The new teacher

1   Read this extract from *Historia de una Maestra* by Josefina Aldecoa.

> Eran unos treinta. Me miraban inexpresivos, callados. En primera fila estaban los pequeños, sentados en el suelo. Detrás, en bancos con pupitres, los medianos. Y al fondo, de pie, los mayores. Treinta niños entre seis y catorce años, indicaba la lista que había encontrado sobre la mesa. Escuela unitaria, mixta, así rezaba mi destino. Yo les sonreí. «Soy la nueva maestra», dije, como si alguno lo ignorara, como si no hubieran estado el día antes acechando mi llegada. Recordaba al más alto, el del fondo. Parecía tener más de catorce años. Estaba medio subido a un árbol, cuando pasé ante él. Ahora me miraba en silencio. Le pregunté: «Eres el mayor, ¿verdad?». Negó con la cabeza y señaló a una niña más pequeña en apariencia.

Answer the following questions in **English**.

(a) Where were the little ones in the class?

....   **(1 mark)**

(b) Where were the older ones?

....   **(1 mark)**

(c) How old were the children?

....   **(1 mark)**

(d) How did the new teacher try to put the children at their ease?

....   **(1 mark)**

(e) What did she conclude about the age of the tall boy?

....   **(1 mark)**

(f) How did the boy respond when she asked if he was the eldest?

....   **(1 mark)**

A charity event

2   Translate this passage into **English**.

> El viernes pasado fui con mis padres a un concurso organizado por la iglesia para recaudar fondos para las víctimas del terremoto. Había cuatro personas en cada equipo y tuvimos que contestar preguntas sobre deportes, geografía, música y las recientes noticias. No ganamos, pero fue una tarde muy entretenida y recaudaron más de ciento cincuenta euros.

....

....

....

....

....

....   **(9 marks)**

Practice test: Reading 4

Problemas medioambientales

1 Lee esta página web de un grupo ecologista sobre problemas en los meses recientes.

Mayo	Arrestaron a un hombre en el Caribe acusado de robar una tortuga gigante de las Islas Galápagos y guardarla en el jardín de su casa. Estas tortugas son una especie amenazada y están bajo la protección de la ley.
Julio	Un líquido peligroso que escapó de una fábrica química se encontró en el agua potable de cientos de casas en el pueblo de Martorell. Los habitantes protestaron delante del ayuntamiento sobre los riesgos de vivir al lado de esta fábrica.
Septiembre	Otro verano sin lluvias ha dejado a muchas regiones en un estado avanzado de sequía. La tierra está amarilla y seca y muchos granjeros han visto las frutas y verduras devastadas.
Noviembre	El gobierno reveló que el uso de energía ha subido otra vez y ha dedicado más dinero a la investigación de recursos naturales sostenibles para reemplazar el carbón y el petróleo.

¿Qué pasó en cada mes?

A	Las tormentas e intensas lluvias han causado inundaciones.
B	Varios hogares se vieron afectados por la contaminación industrial.
C	Descubrieron un animal protegido usado como mascota.
D	Anunciaron otro aumento en el uso de la electricidad.
E	Los agricultores perdieron muchos cultivos.
F	Cerraron una fábrica contaminante por no cumplir con la legislación europea.

Escribe la letra correcta en cada casilla.

(a) Mayo ☐ **(1 mark)**

(b) Julio ☐ **(1 mark)**

(c) Septiembre ☐ **(1 mark)**

(d) Noviembre ☐ **(1 mark)**

Practice test: Reading 5

Food preferences

1   You read these entries in an online forum about favourite food.

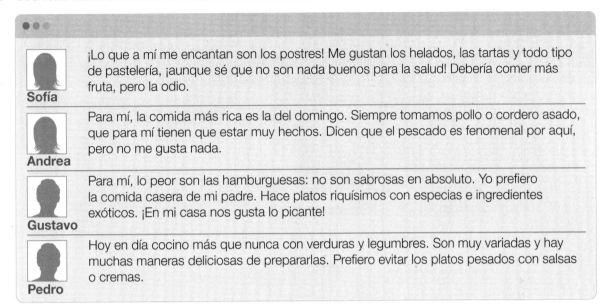

Sofía: ¡Lo que a mí me encantan son los postres! Me gustan los helados, las tartas y todo tipo de pastelería, ¡aunque sé que no son nada buenos para la salud! Debería comer más fruta, pero la odio.

Andrea: Para mí, la comida más rica es la del domingo. Siempre tomamos pollo o cordero asado, que para mí tienen que estar muy hechos. Dicen que el pescado es fenomenal por aquí, pero no me gusta nada.

Gustavo: Para mí, lo peor son las hamburguesas: no son sabrosas en absoluto. Yo prefiero la comida casera de mi padre. Hace platos riquísimos con especias e ingredientes exóticos. ¡En mi casa nos gusta lo picante!

Pedro: Hoy en día cocino más que nunca con verduras y legumbres. Son muy variadas y hay muchas maneras deliciosas de prepararlas. Prefiero evitar los platos pesados con salsas o cremas.

Which food does each person prefer?

A	roast dinners
B	cakes and puddings
C	fruit
D	home cooking
E	vegetables
F	fish and seafood

Write the correct letter in each box.

(a) Sofía   ☐   **(1 mark)**

(b) Isabel   ☐   **(1 mark)**

(c) Gustavo   ☐   **(1 mark)**

(d) Pedro   ☐   **(1 mark)**

Practice test: Writing 1

La familia

1 Estás de intercambio en España con esta familia.

Decides colgar esta foto en Facebook.

Escribe **cuatro** frases en **español** que describan la foto.

(a) .... **(2 marks)**

(b) .... **(2 marks)**

(c) .... **(2 marks)**

(d) .... **(2 marks)**

Reservando alojamiento

2 Vas de vacaciones a España con tu familia.

Escribe una carta al hotel para hacer la reserva.

Menciona:

- duración de la visita
- día y hora de llegada
- habitaciones – detalles
- las comidas que quieres

Escribe aproximadamente **40** palabras en **español**.

Estimado señor:

....

....

....

....

Atentamente,   **(16 marks)**

Practice test: Writing 2

In the restaurant

1 Translate the following sentences into **Spanish**.

I like fish.

me gusta~~~~ el pescado ✓ (correction: el above)

The food here is very good.

la comida aqui es ~~muy~~ bien (correction: buena above)

I am not going to have ice cream, I prefer fruit.

no voy a tomar el helado, prefiero la fruta ✓

I ate in a French restaurant last week.

Comé en un restaurantick de Francia ~~el otro pasado~~ la semana pasada (correction: francés above)

I never eat meat because I am a vegetarian.

nunca como ~~es~~ el carne porque soy vegetariano ✓✓

(10 marks)

Languages

2 Translate the following passage into **Spanish**.

> In my school the Spanish classes are fun and varied and we learn a lot about the language and the country. It is very useful to know another language because it gives you more opportunities to find a well-paid job. I started Spanish when I was eleven and in the future I would like to learn Italian too.

En mi instituto, las ~~estes~~ clases del Español son divertidas y variadas y aprendemos
mucho sobre la lengua y el país. Es muy útil saber otras lenguas (corrections: El idioma / otro idioma above)
porque te da más oportunidades para encontrar un trabajo ~~buen~~ (corrections: de / bien above)
~~estapados~~ pagado. Empezé Español cuando tenía once años y (correction: EprEmpecé con el above)
en el futuro me gustaría aprender Italiano además / también

(12 marks)

117

Practice test: Writing 3

Visitando una ciudad

1   Tu amiga Patricia viene a visitarte y llega mañana.

Escríbele un correo electrónico.

Menciona:

- tus planes para visitar una ciudad el fin de semana
- cómo vais a viajar
- lo que podéis hacer allí
- el tiempo que hizo ayer.

Escribe aproximadamente **90** palabras en **español**.

....

....

....

....

....

....

....

....

....

....

....

....

....

....

....

....

....

....

.... **(16 marks)**

Practice test: Writing 4

Las ambiciones para el futuro

1 Tu amigo Álvaro quiere saber tus planes para el futuro.

Escríbele una carta.

Menciona:

- tus opciones a los dieciséis años
- la experiencia laboral que has tenido.

Escribe aproximadamente **150** palabras en **español**. Responde a los dos aspectos de la pregunta.

....

....

....

....

....

....

....

....

....

....

....

....

....

....

....

....

....

....

....

....

....

(32 marks)

Answers

Identity and culture

1. Physical descriptions
1 B, C, F
2 (a) nose
   (b) hair
   (c) beard
   (d) mouth

2. Character descriptions
1 (a) Alicia
   (b) Dani
   (c) Lucas
   (d) Dani
   (e) Alicia
   (f) Óscar
2 (a) Cuando era joven era un poco tímido/a y muy serio/a.
   (b) Ahora soy más seguro/a de mí mismo/a.
   (c) Soy una persona optimista.
   (d) Mis amigos dicen que soy simpático/a.
   (e) Mis padres piensan que soy perezoso/a.

3. Describing family
1 (a) Diego
   (b) Diego and Pablo / his father
   (c) Lucía
   (d) Rosa
   (e) Ana
2 C, D, F, H

4. Friends
1 (a) C
   (b) A
   (c) A
   (d) C
2 *Sample answer / transcript*

Listen to the recording

¿Qué hay en la foto?

En la foto hay un grupo de jóvenes. Hay chicos y chicas y todos son buenos amigos. Creo que tienen quince o dieciséis años. Parecen muy felices y contentos.

¿Qué tipo de amigo/a eres?

Creo que soy un buen amigo porque escucho a mis amigos y trato de ayudar si tienen problemas. Soy una persona tolerante y me llevo bien con mis amigos.

¿Cómo sería tu amigo o amiga ideal?

Para mí, el amigo ideal tendría un buen sentido del humor. También sería importante tener cosas en común y hacer actividades juntos. El amigo ideal tendría que guardar tus secretos.

¿Cómo es tu mejor amigo o amiga?

Es bastante alto con el pelo moreno. Es divertido y alegre, pero puede ser tonto a veces. No es serio ni responsable, pero es muy inteligente.

¿Qué actividades hiciste con tus amigos el fin de semana pasado?

Jugamos al fútbol en el parque y después salimos al cine. El domingo fuimos al polideportivo para jugar al bádminton y más tarde fuimos de pesca.

5. Relationships
1 (a) P
   (b) N
   (c) N
   (d) P+N
   (e) P+N

2 **Role play**
   Sample answer / transcript

Listen to the recording

Intro: Estás hablando con la amiga de tu amiga española. La amiga os invita a salir.

Teacher: ¿Tú y Miranda queréis salir con nosotros el sábado?

Student: Miranda no puede ir porque está ocupada el sábado.

Teacher: ¿Y tú, entonces? ¿Quieres salir conmigo y unos amigos?

Student: Sí, me gustaría mucho. No quiero pasar el día solo/sola.

Teacher: ¿Adónde prefieres ir? ¿A la playa o a la montaña?

Student: Prefiero ir a la playa porque va a hacer muy buen tiempo.

Teacher: ¿Cómo te llevas con Miranda?

Student: Me llevo muy bien con ella.

Teacher: Pues fantástico.

Student: ¿Cómo es tu relación con Miranda?

Teacher: Somos buenas amigas.. Es como mi hermana.

6. Marriage and partnership
1 (a) B
   (b) F
   (c) H
   (d) D
2 (a) Pablo: P, N
   (b) Cristina: P+N, N

7. When I was younger
1 (a) He was an only child.
   (b) (i) a desert island in the sea (ii) a tropical (rain) forest with wild animals
   (c) He didn't get good grades.
   (d) He read a lot and he wrote (little) stories.
2 B, D, E

8. Social media
1 (a) B
   (b) A
   (c) D
   (d) C
   (e) B
   (f) C
2 **Model answer:** Me gusta usar las redes sociales para ver lo que hacen mis amigos y mirar las fotos que cuelgan. También algunos de los vídeos son realmente divertidos. A veces pueden ser peligrosas porque algunas personas mienten sobre su edad y quiénes son. Nunca organizaría reunirme con alguien que conocí en Internet. Anoche usé una red social para jugar un juego durante veinte minutos y cuando hacía mis deberes, escribí una pregunta en la página de mi clase de geografía.

Este sábado voy a subir unas fotos de mis últimas vacaciones.

9. Technology

1. (a) C   (d) B

   (b) A   (e) A

   (c) D

2. **Role play**

   Sample answer / transcript

   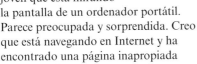

   Listen to the recording

   Intro: Estás hablando de tecnología con tu amigo español.

   Teacher: ¿Cómo usas la tecnología?

   Student: Descargo música.

   Teacher: ¿Qué piensas de las tabletas?

   Student: Son un poco grandes para llevar.

   Teacher: ¿Te gusta jugar a juegos en Internet? ¿Por qué?

   Student: Sí, bastante. Puede ser relajante.

   Teacher: A mí también. ¿Qué piensas del coste de la tecnología?

   Student: Creo que es muy cara.

   Teacher: Es verdad.

   Student: ¿Cuál es tu página web favorita?

   Teacher: Una de mapas. Son muy útiles.

10. The internet

1. (a) B, E

   (b) to play educational games and watch children's videos

2. (a) A   (c) F

   (b) C   (d) H

3. I can't imagine life without the internet because in my house we usually use it every day. If you forget the name of a film or you want to know when a certain author was born, the internet has all the answers. Furthermore / In addition, it has changed the way in which we do our shopping / the way we shop.

11. Pros and cons of technology

1. (a) C   (c) B

   (b) B   (d) A

2. *Sample answer / transcript*

   ¿Qué hay en la foto?

   Listen to the recording

   En la foto hay una niña joven que está mirando la pantalla de un ordenador portátil. Parece preocupada y sorprendida. Creo que está navegando en Internet y ha encontrado una página inapropiada para pequeños.

   ¿Qué problemas hay con Internet?

   Es fácil pasar demasiado tiempo en Internet cuando deberíamos estar haciendo cosas más activas o creativas. Hay problemas con la piratería y el fraude y personas que no son quienes dicen que son. También, el acoso cibernético es muy desagradable para las víctimas.

   ¿Cuáles son los aspectos buenos de Internet?

   Internet nos permite mantenernos en contacto con amigos y parientes y es una fuente casi infinita de información. Con Internet la comunicación es rápida y fácil y puedes ahorrar tiempo y dinero haciendo las compras en la red.

   ¿Qué hiciste en Internet anoche?

   Anoche descargué unas canciones, mandé un ensayo a mi profesor por correo electrónico y charlé con mis amigos en la red. Fue muy útil porque organizamos un partido de fútbol.

   ¿Cómo vas a usar Internet este fin de semana?

   Este fin de semana voy a usar unos sitios web que me ayudan a repasar para los exámenes. También jugaré a unos juegos en mi tiempo libre. Probablemente buscaré información para mis deberes el domingo.

12. Hobbies

1. (a) A   (d) B

   (b) D   (e) A

   (c) C

2. **Model answer:** En mi tiempo libre hago atletismo y juego al tenis. También me gusta tocar la guitarra y dibujar. Hago atletismo los sábados y juego al tenis los domingos con mi hermano. Me gustan los deportes porque son emocionantes y muy activos. Mis otros pasatiempos son relajantes y creativos.

13. Music

1. (a) C   (d) B

   (b) B   (e) C

   (c) D   (f) A

2. (a) One of: He came here to study music / to improve his art (skills) / to get better opportunities.

   (b) (i) Breakfast is the best meal of the day. (ii) One of: He has lots of fans. / He is having some success. / He has met some good musicians.

   (c) (i) He plays and writes songs. (ii) He has a rest and goes out.

   (d) His ideas for songs won't let him.

   (e) He does a concert or radio appearance.

   (f) to promote his music

14. Music events

1. (a) C   (d) B

   (b) D   (e) D

   (c) A   (f) C

2. F, B, C

15. Sport

1. (a) C   (c) C

   (b) B   (d) A

2. B, C, E

16. Sporting events

1. (a) scored a goal

   (b) heads down

   (c) The boys were watching them.

   (d) one nil

   (e) They were much better than theirs/hers.

   (f) that she should calm down / that there was plenty of time left

2. (a) A   (b) C   (c) B

17. Films

1. (a) Screen 2: E

   (b) Screen 3: C

   (c) Screen 4: A

2   (a) She has to study.

(b) Her parents won't let her.

(c) They had a good time at the cinema. / They laughed a lot.

(d) the best moments of the film

(e) She did a dramatic impersonation of the leading actress.

18. TV

1   A, C, H, E

2   (a) films   (c) soaps

(b) documentaries   (d) boring

3   **Model answer:** Me gusta ver la televisión por la tarde cuando termino mis deberes. Es una buena manera de relajarme.

Esta noche voy a ver una serie policíaca que es muy emocionante y, después, una película cómica. Probablemente veré las noticias con mi familia porque es importante saber lo que está pasando en el mundo.

No me gustan nada los realitys/los programas de telerrealidad porque no son interesantes y detesto los concursos porque la gente es muy tonta.

Cuando era menor me gustaban mucho los dibujos animados. Pensaba que eran muy divertidos y los veía cada día cuando volvía de la escuela.

19. Food and drink

1   (a) sandwich   (c) omelette

(b) strawberry   (d) pineapple

2   (a) E   (c) D

(b) A   (d) C

3   I really like going out for tapas because you can try a variety of dishes. In Galicia, where I live, the speciality is fish and last night I had seafood in a very tasty sauce. This weekend we are going out for dinner with my grandparents and I shall have a steak.

20. Eating in a café

1   (a) D   (b) C   (c) H

2   **Role play**

Sample answer / transcript

Intro: Estás con tu amigo en una cafetería y pides algo para beber y comer.

Teacher: ¿Qué quieres tomar?

Student: Quiero un café con leche.

Teacher: ¿Quieres comer algo?

Student: Me gustaría una hamburguesa.

Teacher: ¿Qué bebes normalmente cuando estás en casa?

Student: Bebo zumo de naranja.

Teacher: ¿Qué piensas de la comida española?

Student: Es muy rica.

Teacher: Me alegro.

Student: ¿Cuánto cuesta?

Teacher: Nada. Te invito yo.

3   **Model answer:** En la foto mi hermana está en un café. Está con sus amigos. Mi hermana está tomando un café. Su amigo está tomando un zumo de naranja y su amiga está tomando un té.

21. Eating in a restaurant

1   (a) salad   (d) peach

(b) (potato) omelette   (e) chicken

(c) spaghetti

2   D, E, G

22. Meals at home

1   (a) I have / she has been a vegetarian for 5 years.

(b) I have / he has just prepared a fish soup.

(c) We / they always sit at the table to eat.

(d) I have not / he has not drunk coffee for 2 years.

2   *Sample answer / transcript*

Listen to the recording

¿Qué hay en la foto?

En la foto hay una familia comiendo en torno a la mesa en la cocina. Son el padre, la madre y sus dos hijos, un niño y una niña. Están tomando pollo con ensalada y pan. Están bebiendo agua. Es una comida sana y la familia está contenta.

¿Qué es una comida típica en tu casa?

Una comida típica en mi casa son los espaguetis con salsa boloñesa. Es un plato italiano, pero es muy popular en este país también. Mi padre lo hace muchas veces el viernes porque es rápido y sabroso.

¿Qué tomaste para comer el fin de semana pasado?

El sábado pasado comimos filete con ensalada y patatas fritas, pero no comimos postre. Estaba muy rico. El domingo tomamos albóndigas con arroz y judías verdes. De postre había una tarta de manzana deliciosa.

¿A qué hora tomáis las comidas en casa?

En mi casa tomamos el desayuno sobre las siete y media y la cena a eso de las seis. Los fines de semana solemos desayunar más tarde y comer sobre la una.

¿Qué tal la comida en tu instituto?

En mi instituto la comida es bastante aburrida. No hay mucha variedad y no es muy sana. Hay pizza y patatas fritas casi todos los días.

23. Shopping for food

1   (a) on the kitchen table   (e) (the box of) biscuits

(b) half a kilo   (f) 100 grams

(c) market   (g) a can/tin of tuna

(d) bananas

2   **Role play**

Sample answer / transcript

Listen to the recording

Intro: Estás comprando comida en una tienda en Tarragona. Hablas con el dependiente.

Teacher: Buenos días. ¿En qué puedo ayudarle?

Student: Quiero unas fresas.

Teacher: ¿Cuántos kilos quiere?

Student: Deme medio kilo.

Teacher: Muy bien. ¿Algo más?

Student: Sí, una botella de agua mineral.

Teacher: Aquí tiene.

Student: También quiero cuatro lonchas de queso.

Teacher: Muy bien. ¿Eso es todo?

Student: Sí, ¿cuánto es?

Teacher: Cuatro con veinte.

24. Opinions about food

1 (a) A   (d) B

  (b) A   (e) C

  (c) C

2 Me gusta mucho la comida española y el restaurante cerca de la iglesia hace comida buenísima. El pescado es muy rico / sabroso y me encantó la salchicha picante que tomé / comí la semana pasada. La comida siempre es apetitosa y, en mi opinión, es bastante sana. Vamos a comer allí el viernes y probaré el marisco.

25. Celebrations

1 (a) C   (d) C

  (b) B   (e) D

  (c) A   (f) B

2 (a) C   (b) A   (c) G

26. Customs

1 (a) A   (c) A

  (b) B   (d) B

2 *Sample answer / transcript*

¿Qué hay en la foto?

Hay una familia al aire libre y hay un fuego porque es el cinco de noviembre, que es una fiesta en Gran Bretaña. Hay fuegos artificiales y un ambiente alegre.

¿Qué costumbre has celebrado en tu casa en el último año?

En octubre tuvimos una fiesta para Halloween y todos nos disfrazamos de fantasmas o esqueletos. Contamos historias de terror, vimos una película de miedo y comimos hamburguesas y perritos calientes.

¿Qué tipo de comida prefieres para una ocasión especial?

Me gusta mucho la comida italiana y para mi cumpleaños vamos a mi restaurante favorito para tomar pasta y bistec.

¿Qué piensas de las costumbres españolas?

Creo que las fiestas españolas son muy animadas y divertidas. También pienso que son bastante caras.

¿Crees que la siesta es una buena idea para tu país?

No, creo que la siesta no es una buena idea para mi país porque no hace calor aquí como en España y solo tenemos una hora para comer.

27. Spanish festivals

1 (a) She protects / looks after everyone associated with the sea, even swimmers and windsurfers.

  (b) to the port / harbour

  (c) in a boat decorated with lights and flowers

  (d) on a trip round the bay

  (e) music and a procession of boats

2 B, F, G

28. South American festivals

1 (a) cena especial

  (b) ropa tradicional

  (c) fuegos artificiales

  (d) platos típicos

2 B, D, F, H

Local, national, international and global areas of interest

29. Describing a region

1 A, D, G

2 **Role play**

Sample answer / transcript

Intro: Estás hablando con tu amigo español sobre dónde vives.

Teacher: ¿Cómo es tu ciudad?

Student: Es bastante bonita, pero hay partes sucias.

Teacher: ¿Sabes algo de la historia de tu región?

Student: Lo más importante en el pasado de la ciudad fue la industria de la lana.

Teacher: ¿Qué piensas de vivir aquí? … ¿Por qué?

Student: Me gusta vivir aquí porque mi familia y mis amigos viven cerca.

Teacher: ¿Y la industria en tu región?

Student: Hay una fábrica de coches y muchas empresas pequeñas.

Teacher: Muy bien.

Student: ¿Cuántos habitantes hay en tu ciudad?

Teacher: Hay unos quinientos mil.

30. Describing a town

1 (a) B   (d) C

  (b) C   (e) B

  (c) A

2 **Model answer:** La ciudad empezó a prosperar a principios del siglo veinte con las minas de carbón y la industria textil, sobre todo el algodón.

Hoy la gente trabaja en las tiendas en el centro o en la gran fábrica de comida en las afueras. Algunas personas viajan a las grandes ciudades cerca de aquí para trabajar.

En la ciudad necesitamos más actividades para los jóvenes y me gustaría tener una bolera y un parque de monopatín.

Hay varios parques y jardines bonitos que están llenos de flores y árboles.

31. Places to see

1 (a) just out of town; a 20-minute walk away

  (b) It's one of the oldest in the country.

  (c) It was voted best in the north.

  (d) what life was like a hundred years ago

  (e) behind the town hall

  (f) to the left of the library

2 *Sample answer / transcript*

Listen to the recording

¿Qué hay en la foto?

Hay una ciudad. Está en la costa y tiene edificios muy altos. También hay una plaza de toros y barcos en el puerto. Se ve el mar y hay árboles en las montañas.

¿Qué piensas de visitar ciudades en otros países?

Es muy interesante. Las tiendas son diferentes y me gusta visitar los monumentos.

¿Qué visitaste en tus últimas vacaciones?

Fui a Londres un fin de semana y visité el castillo de Buckingham. También fui al teatro para ver un espectáculo de música y fui en barco por el río.

¿Adónde van los turistas cuando visitan tu región?

Van a las ciudades grandes para experimentar la cultura y visitar los museos y galerías. También van a las montañas y los lagos.

¿Te gusta tu barrio? … ¿Por qué (no)?

No, no me gusta mucho porque es muy aburrido y no hay nada que hacer.

32. Places to visit

1 (a) B (d) C
(b) C (e) C
(c) A

2 **Model answer:** En mi ciudad hay un gran mercado dos veces por semana, una gran variedad de tiendas y un centro comercial popular. Hay muchas pequeñas calles en el barrio histórico con edificios antiguos y cafés bonitos.

Durante el día, se puede dar un paseo en el parque o hacer una excursión en bicicleta al lado del río.

Por la noche, se puede ir al cine o cenar en uno de los restaurantes. También hay conciertos en el teatro.

Hace dos semanas hicimos una excursión con el instituto para visitar el zoo. Tuvimos una presentación para explicar el trabajo de conservación del zoo y vimos todos los animales.

33. The weather

1 (a) D (d) A
(b) D (e) C
(c) B

2 I live in the north-west of Spain and the climate here is not as hot as in the south. In summer the weather is good with pleasant temperatures but the sun does not shine every day. We have had a rainy weekend and tomorrow it will be quite windy.

34. Shopping

1 (a) M (c) M+E
(b) E (d) M+E

2 (a) too small
(b) She looks in the windows and thinks.
(c) from a catalogue / by mail order

3 Role play

Sample answer / transcript

Listen to the recording

Intro: Estás con tu amiga española y te pregunta qué quieres hacer.

Teacher: ¿Qué quieres hacer este sábado?

Student: Me gustaría ir de compras. Quiero comprar unas cosas para mi familia.

Teacher: ¿Adónde quieres ir de compras? … ¿Por qué?

Student: Prefiero ir a un centro comercial porque hay mucha variedad.

Teacher: ¿Qué vas a comprar?

Student: Voy a comprar una pulsera y unos guantes.

Teacher: ¿A qué hora vamos?

Student: A las diez.

Teacher: Entonces vamos al centro comercial en la ciudad.

Student: ¿Te gusta ir de compras?

Teacher: Me encanta.

35. Buying gifts

1 (a) B (d) B
(b) C (e) B
(c) A

2 (a) C (d) D
(b) B (e) A
(c) D (f) C

36. Money

1 (a) parents and other family members
(b) It has gone up more than 50% (compared to other times).
(c) entertainment activities
(d) Parents and grandparents are buying more products for the children.
(e) One of: They have more money/income to spend on these items. / They are pressurised to buy more.

2 Role play

Sample answer / transcript

Listen to the recording

Intro: Estás hablando con tu amigo sobre el dinero.

Teacher: ¿Cuánto dinero recibes como paga?

Student: Recibo quince libras a la semana.

Teacher: ¿Quién te da el dinero y cuándo?

Student: Mis padres y mi abuela me lo dan cada viernes.

Teacher: ¿Cuánto dinero intentas ahorrar?

Student: Normalmente pongo tres libras en el banco.

Teacher: ¿Qué te gusta comprar con tu dinero?

Student: Suelo comprar revistas y caramelos.

Teacher: Yo también.

Student: ¿Piensas que recibes bastante paga?

Teacher: Sí, estoy contento con mi paga.

37. Charities

1
(a) C   (d) A

(b) C   (e) B

(c) B   (f) C

2 **Role play**

Sample answer / transcript

Listen to the recording

TRACK 109

Intro: Estás hablando con tu amigo sobre los eventos benéficos en tu instituto.

Teacher: ¿Para qué asociaciones organizas eventos benéficos en tu instituto?

Student: Muchas veces recaudamos dinero para ayudar con la investigación científica de ciertas enfermedades y en otras ocasiones nos gusta ayudar a causas medioambientales.

Teacher: ¿Qué tipo de actividades organizas?

Student: Hemos organizado un baile para los padres y profesores para recaudar fondos y también un concierto de música con la orquesta y el coro.

Teacher: ¿Cuánto dinero recaudan en general?

Student: Depende de la actividad, pero normalmente entre ochenta y ciento veinte libras.

Teacher: No está mal. ¿Cuál es el beneficio para el individuo, en tu opinión?

Student: Aprendes nuevas habilidades como el trabajo en equipo y la contabilidad.

Teacher: Sí, es verdad.

Student: ¿Cuál es tu organización benéfica favorita y por qué?

Teacher: Me gusta ayudar a Oxfam porque hacen mucho trabajo para ayudar en países muy pobres.

38. Volunteering

1
(a) A   (d) B

(b) C   (e) D

(c) D

2 *Sample answer / transcript*

¿Qué hay en la foto?

Listen to the recording

TRACK 110

Es una foto de un grupo de personas que limpian la playa. Hay dos adultos y cuatro niños. Quitan la basura y la ponen en bolsas. Hace sol, pero no mucho calor porque llevan chaquetas.

¿Cuáles son los beneficios del trabajo voluntario?

Hay muchos beneficios para la sociedad y también para el individuo. Muchas personas reciben ayuda, como la gente pobre o los ancianos, y también hay muchos beneficios para el medio ambiente.

¿Qué experiencia de trabajo voluntario has tenido?

El año pasado trabajé varios fines de semana en una tienda con fines benéficos. Recibía las bolsas de ropa y libros que la gente llevaba y organizaba las cosas en la tienda. También servía a los clientes.

¿Qué oportunidades hay para el trabajo voluntario en tu ciudad?

Siempre hay la oportunidad de ayudar en una residencia de ancianos o en una de las escuelas primarias. También de vez en cuando hay una operación para limpiar el río o quitar la basura del bosque.

¿Cuál es tu opinión sobre hacer trabajo voluntario? … ¿Por qué?

Aprendes varias habilidades que puedes utilizar en el mundo laboral. Por ejemplo, cómo relacionarte con la gente, cómo ser un miembro efectivo del equipo y cómo responder a las quejas de los clientes.

39. Helping others

1
(a) E   (c) C

(b) F   (d) G

2 **Model answer:**

En la foto una mujer está secando un plato.

Su hija está lavando los platos.

Las dos tienen el pelo largo.

Hay muchos platos sucios.

40. Healthy living

1
(a) F   (c) N

(b) P   (d) P

2
(a) chicken with carrots

(b) prawns with rice

(c) omelette with ham

41. Unhealthy living

1
(a) bottles, glasses and packets

(b) (a cocktail of) red wine and coca cola/coke

(c) to get drunk

(d) They are smoking joints.

(e) the noise and the rubbish

(f) Not much, because it reappears somewhere else the next weekend.

2
(a) Los jóvenes nunca deben fumar.

(b) Deberías resistir la tentación de drogarte/ tomar drogas.

(c) Tengo que cuidar el/mi corazón.

(d) Mi hermano debería perder unos kilos.

(e) Mis padres solo beben alcohol con moderación.

42. Peer group pressure

1
(a) H   (d) C

(b) A   (e) J

(c) B   (f) G

2 **Model answer:** Mi amiga Claire es pequeña, delgada y morena con el pelo largo y liso. Es bastante tímida y no está muy segura de sí misma. Por eso, quiso ser más atrevida y empezó a salir con un grupo de chicas mayores un poco tontas. Descubrí que bebía mucho alcohol cuando salía con sus nuevas amigas y que se comportaba muy mal. Intenté hablar con ella y decirle la verdad sobre las chicas que eran sus amigas. Por suerte, me escuchó. Este fin de semana vamos a salir juntas. Comeremos pizza y después iremos a un concierto.

43. Green issues

1
(a) A   (d) B

(b) C   (e) A

(c) D   (f) D

2 H, C, F, E

44. Natural resources

1 (a) A   (d) A
  (b) C   (e) A
  (c) C   (f) B

2 *Sample answer / transcript*

Listen to the recording

¿Qué hay en la foto?

En la foto hay un chico que usa el contenedor de su instituto para reciclar las botellas de plástico.

¿Qué se hace en tu instituto para ayudar el medio ambiente?

Tenemos que apagar las luces y los ordenadores al final del día. También se debe evitar el malgasto del papel escribiendo en los dos lados.

¿Qué has reciclado en casa el mes pasado?

Hemos reciclado los restos de comida, el plástico, las latas, el vidrio y el cartón. Tenemos contenedores separados para todas estas cosas.

¿Cómo se puede evitar el malgasto del agua?

Tienes que cerrar el grifo cuando te cepillas los dientes, ducharte en lugar de bañarte y usar el agua de lluvia en las plantas y las flores.

¿Cómo se puede reducir el uso de electricidad en casa?

Es importante apagar todos los aparatos eléctricos, como la televisión y la consola de videojuegos. También puedes bajar la calefacción y ponerte un jersey.

45. Environmental action

1 (a) C   (e) D
  (b) A   (f) C
  (c) B   (g) A
  (d) D

2 (a) swimming underwater
  (b) marine animals and birds
  (c) fishermen and tourists
  (d) plastic bottles and containers
  (e) They end up trapped in bottles.

46. Global issues

1 (a) Are they the poorest in the village?
  (b) There are worse things.
  (c) He is in prison.
  (d) if he has killed someone
  (e) He will die because he can't breathe.
  (f) leaving the sick man on his own

2 (a) A   (c) G
  (b) D   (d) B

47. Poverty

1 (a) E   (d) H
  (b) B   (e) D
  (c) A

2 Me preocupa que haya tanta pobreza en mi país. Hay muchos niños que no tienen suficiente comida / suficiente para comer. Viven en casas sin calefacción y en invierno pasan frío y hambre. Esta Navidad, en mi clase, vamos a reunir mantas y comida para llevar a familias necesitadas. Ayer llevé algunas latas y paquetes al instituto.

48. Homelessness

1 (a) B   (c) C
  (b) B   (d) A

2 *Sample answer / transcript*

Listen to the recording

¿Qué hay en la foto?

En la foto hay un hombre sin techo sentado en el suelo, en la calle. Hace frío y el hombre lleva una gorra y guantes. También hay una chica joven y le está dando un regalo al hombre. Es una caja cubierta de papel.

¿Cuál sería el regalo ideal para un hombre sin techo?

Creo que lo más útil sería ropa de lana o una manta contra el frío. También una buena idea sería latas de comida o una almohada.

¿Cuál es el problema principal para las personas sin techo?

Depende de dónde viven. Si es en un país del norte, el frío sería lo peor sobre todo en invierno y por la noche. En países más cálidos, el hambre sería lo más difícil porque nunca tienen suficiente para comer.

¿Cómo has ayudado a los sin techo en el pasado?

Hemos reunido ropa vieja incluyendo abrigos, guantes y bufandas para distribuir entre los sin techo de nuestra ciudad. También varias veces hemos preparado sopa y bocadillos para ellos.

¿Por qué piensas que los sin techo están en esta situación?

Creo que hay muchas razones. En el caso de algunos, tienen una historia de drogas y alcohol y han perdido la capacidad de cuidarse. Pero para otros, es una cuestión de mala suerte, de desempleo, de tener padres violentos y muchas otras razones.

49. Countries and nationalities

1 (a) H   (e) F
  (b) D   (f) I
  (c) C   (g) A
  (d) B

2 (a) G   (c) A
  (b) D   (d) F

50. Tourist information

1 (a) a (street) map of the town
  (b) next to the church
  (c) the other side of the bridge
  (d) It opens at ten.
  (e) the times the boat trips go; the routes they follow
  (f) a guided tour of the town

2 **Role play**

Sample answer / transcript

Listen to the recording

Intro: Hablas con la empleada en la Oficina de Turismo.

Teacher: Buenos días. ¿En qué puedo ayudarle?

Student: Quisiera información sobre los sitios de interés en la ciudad.

Teacher: Aquí tiene.

Student: También me gustaría una lista de alojamientos.

Teacher: Muy bien. ¿Qué tipo de alojamiento prefiere usted?

Student: Quiero un hotel barato.

Teacher: Aquí tiene una lista de hoteles. ¿Algo más?

Student: Sí, necesito un horario de trenes.

Teacher: Lo siento, no tenemos. Hay que ir a la oficina de Renfe.

Student: ¿Dónde está la estación?

Teacher: Enfrente del ayuntamiento.

51. Accommodation

1 (a) C   (d) A
  (b) A   (e) D
  (c) B

2 (a) campsite in Italy
  (b) cousin's house / house in Barcelona
  (c) youth hostel in the country
  (d) hotel on the coast

52. Hotels

1 (a) B   (d) A
  (b) D   (e) C
  (c) A

2 (a) himself, his wife and two children
  (b) It's cheaper and the room is bigger.
  (c) A, D, F, H
  (d) one

53. Camping

1 (a) C   (c) A
  (b) A   (d) B

2 Role play

Sample answer / transcript

Listen to the recording

SPEAKING TRACK 114

Intro: Estás hablando por teléfono con el empleado del camping y quieres reservar una parcela.

Teacher: Buenos días. ¿En qué puedo ayudarle?

Student: Quisiera reservar una parcela en el camping para cuatro personas y una tienda.

Teacher: ¿Para cuántas noches y en qué fechas?

Student: Para diez noches. Vamos a llegar el 30 de julio.

Teacher: Muy bien. ¿Algo más?

Student: Sí. ¿Es posible alquilar bicicletas en el camping?

Teacher: Sí, hay una oficina al lado de la recepción. ¿Cuál es su nacionalidad?

Student: Soy inglés/inglesa.

Teacher: De acuerdo.

Student: ¿Qué instalaciones hay en el camping?

Teacher: Les mandaré un folleto con todos los detalles. Gracias.

54. Holiday preferences

1 A, C, E, G

2 (a) C   (d) B
  (b) A
  (c) B

55. Holiday destinations

1 (a) D   (d) D
  (b) C   (e) C
  (c) B

2 (a) coast   (d) country(side)
  (b) city / town   (e) theme park
  (c) mountains

56. Travelling

1 (a) the station
  (b) give him a lift / pick him up
  (c) buy her a ticket
  (d) His train is delayed.
  (e) change trains twice
  (f) during the day

2 Role play

Sample answer / transcript

Listen to the recording

SPEAKING TRACK 115

Intro: Llamas a tu amigo para confirmar los detalles de tu visita a su casa.

Teacher: ¿Cuándo vas a llegar?

Student: Voy a llegar el diez de agosto a las once.

Teacher: ¿Cuáles son los detalles de tu llegada?

Student: Viajo en tren y llego a la estación en el centro.

Teacher: ¿Qué equipaje tienes?

Student: Tengo una mochila y una bolsa.

Teacher: Vivo bastante lejos de la estación.

Student: ¿Cómo voy a llegar a la casa?

Teacher: Lo mejor sería coger un taxi. ¿Qué quieres hacer el sábado?

Student: Me gustaría ir a la playa.

Teacher: Buena idea.

57. Holiday activities

1 (a) A   (e) A
  (b) B   (f) D
  (c) C   (g) B
  (d) D

2 (a) B   (d) B
  (b) C   (e) B
  (c) A

58. Holiday experiences

1 (a) A, D, F, H
  (b) He missed Spanish food.
  (c) It wasn't very varied.

2 C, D, F, H

59. Transport and directions

1 (a) turn right
  (b) cross the bridge
  (c) the second street on the left
  (d) Church Square / the square
  (e) the post office
  (f) opposite the hairdresser's

2 **Model answer:** Normalmente, cuando hace sol, voy al instituto a pie porque no está muy lejos. Pero si llueve, mi madre me lleva en coche.

Cuando fuimos de vacaciones el año pasado, cogimos el barco del puerto para viajar a Francia. Para el resto del viaje estuvimos en nuestro coche. Es muy práctico tener el coche.

En mi región, los pueblos tienen una red de autobuses para llegar a la ciudad, y en la ciudad los trenes van a todas partes del país. El sistema es bueno.

Para mantenerme en forma voy a ir en bicicleta a las tiendas o a la casa de mis amigos.

60. Transport problems

1 (a) car

(b) petrol

(c) broken-down lorry

(d) He had missed his train.

(e) The door wouldn't close.

2 **Role play**

Sample answer / transcript

Listen to the recording

Intro: Usted está hablando con un policía sobre un accidente que vio.

Teacher: ¿Dónde estaba usted cuando vio el accidente?

Student: Estaba aquí en el cruce, delante de la tienda de comestibles.

Teacher: ¿Qué pasó?

Student: Hubo un accidente entre dos coches.

Teacher: ¿Quién causó el accidente?

Student: Creo que el conductor del coche rojo.

Teacher: Muy bien.

Student: ¿Hay muchos accidentes aquí?

Teacher: No, esta es la primera vez. ¿Me puede dar su dirección aquí en España?

Student: Sí, estoy en el hotel Rocamar en el centro.

Teacher: Gracias por su ayuda.

61. Holiday problems

1 (a) It's too small to sit on.

(b) The heat in the bedroom is unbearable.

(c) The air conditioning is broken.

(d) There are no towels and it's not very clean.

(e) It has nice/pretty gardens and a good restaurant.

(f) by changing apartment

2 (a) La ducha no funciona. / No funciona la ducha.

(b) No hay sábanas en la cama.

(c) Me hacen falta / Me faltan / Necesito dos toallas en el (cuarto de) baño.

(d) Visité la ciudad ayer y perdí mi pasaporte.

(e) El (cuarto de) baño no está muy limpio y falta jabón.

62. Asking for help abroad

1 (a) umbrellas

(b) earrings

(c) mobile phones

(d) keys

(e) watches

2 (a) in her bag / handbag

(b) yesterday evening / last night

(c) black leather

(d) It contains a photo of her husband.

(e) fill in a form

Current and future study and employment

63. School subjects

1 (a) It's very practical.

(b) very boring

(c) easy

(d) interesting

(e) No, because he always gets bad marks. / No, because it's difficult to learn all the dates.

2 *Sample answer / transcript*

Listen to the recording

¿Qué hay en la foto?

En la foto hay tres estudiantes jóvenes, dos chicos y una chica. Están en una clase de informática y el profesor está explicando algo que ven en la pantalla de los ordenadores. Parecen contentos y creo que les gusta la clase.

¿Qué piensas de estudiar informática?

Pienso que es importante estudiar informática porque es muy útil tener conocimiento de ordenadores en el mundo laboral. La gran mayoría de empresas buscan personas familiarizadas con la tecnología.

¿Qué asignaturas te gustaban en el pasado?

Antes me interesaba mucho el arte dramático y era mi asignatura favorita. Me gustaba mucho la profesora y las clases eran muy divertidas y animadas.

¿Cuáles son tus planes para los estudios en el futuro?

Me gustaría estudiar geografía. Será muy interesante aprender sobre la formación de la tierra y hay muchos programas y páginas web útiles que me ayudarán a entender los aspectos difíciles.

¿Qué asignatura te gusta menos y por qué?

No me gustan nada las matemáticas. No las entiendo en absoluto. Odio las clases porque no comprendo las explicaciones de la profesora. Voy a dejar las matemáticas tan pronto como sea posible.

64. Success in school

1 (a) B (d) A

(b) A (e) C

(c) B (f) A

2 Role play

Sample answer / transcript

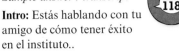

Listen to the recording

Intro: Estás hablando con tu amigo de cómo tener éxito en el instituto..

Teacher: ¿Cuál es la mejor manera de hacer los deberes?

Student: Es importante hacer los deberes cada tarde.

Teacher: ¿Cómo debe comportarse en clase el estudiante ideal?

Student: Debe escuchar al profesor.

Teacher: ¿Qué haces si estás ausente y pierdes clases?

Student: Pido ayuda al profesor el día siguiente.

Teacher: ¿Cómo te preparas para los exámenes?

Student: Hago un plan de repaso.

Teacher: Eso es una buena idea.

Student: Y tú, ¿cómo haces el repaso?

Teacher: Uso las páginas web educativas.

65. School life

1 C, E, F, H

2 Role play

Sample answer / transcript

Listen to the recording

Intro: Estás hablando con tu amigo sobre tu instituto.

Teacher: ¿Qué tipo de deberes tienes que hacer?

Student: A veces tenemos que buscar información en el ordenador y escribir notas.

Teacher: ¿Hay actividades o clubes para los alumnos?

Student: Sí, tenemos muchos. Hay un club de música, otro de arte dramático.

Teacher: ¿Cómo te preparas para los exámenes?

Student: Leo mis notas, practico escribiendo planes para ensayos y repaso con páginas web educativas.

Teacher: Yo también. ¿Cómo es tu uniforme?

Student: No está mal. Llevamos pantalones negros o una falda negra con una camisa blanca, un jersey azul y la corbata del instituto.

Teacher: Muy bien.

Student: ¿Cómo fueron los últimos exámenes?

Teacher: Bastante bien. Saqué buenas notas.

66. The school day

1 (a) A   (d) B
   (b) A   (e) B
   (c) C   (f) C

2 (a) (around) 7.45
   (b) school door/gate
   (c) 20 minutes
   (d) They have free afternoons.
   (e) do sport / have piano lessons / do what they like

67. Comparing schools

1 B, E, D, G

2 (a) They start at nine.
   (b) traffic jams and impatient people
   (c) All the buses and parents in cars arrive at the same time.

(d) registration / the teacher taking the register

(e) drama and business studies

(f) It was early.

(g) They get homework every day.

68. Describing schools

1 (a) C   (d) C
   (b) A   (e) A
   (c) C   (f) B

2 Mi instituto es bastante viejo y tiene muchas aulas, tres laboratorios y un gimnasio. Hace cinco años construyeron una biblioteca grande / una gran biblioteca que es muy moderna y tiene instalaciones buenas. El año que viene / El año próximo van a crear nuevas canchas de tenis.

69. School rules

1 (a) C   (d) A
   (b) D   (e) C
   (c) A   (f) B

2 **Model answer:** En mi instituto no se puede correr en los pasillos, lo que los alumnos pequeños suelen hacer. Otra cosa prohibida es el chicle porque causa manchas desagradables y algunas personas dejan papeles por el suelo.

Los alumnos deben respetar a los profesores y los otros estudiantes y tratar a todos con consideración y cortesía. No se tolera el acoso en absoluto y hay castigos severos.

Hay algunas reglas muy importantes que son esenciales para asegurar el progreso de los alumnos. Por ejemplo, no se permite hablar mientras el profesor está hablando. Esto es muy importante si quieres aprender.

La regla que encuentro estúpida es la necesidad de llevar uniforme. Sobre todo detesto la corbata. Cuando mi profesor me encontró tres veces sin corbata, me puso un montón de deberes extra, incluyendo un ensayo sobre la historia de la corbata.

70. Problems at school

1 (a) C   (e) D
   (b) B   (f) A
   (c) A   (g) D
   (d) B

2 Many students say that there is a high level of pressure in schools in modern society. They think that it is only acceptable to get the best grades and to study the most academic subjects. Some schools have organised sessions after class designed to reduce the stress that they feel. These include swimming, basketball and skateboarding.

71. Primary school

1 A, D, F, H

2 *Sample answer / transcript*

<u>¿Qué hay en la foto?</u>

Listen to the recording

En la foto hay una clase. Se ven a los estudiantes y la profesora. Ella es joven. Tiene el pelo largo y rubio y hace una pregunta. Una chica levanta la mano para contestar. En la pared hay muchos pósteres.

¿Cómo eras de pequeño/a?

Era bastante creativa y siempre quería dibujar o crear cosas artísticas. También me encantaba escribir historias y cantar. Me comportaba bien en la escuela y tenía bastantes amigos.

¿Cómo era tu profesor favorito o profesora favorita?

Un año tuve una profesora bastante mayor que era muy simpática y amable. Era como una abuela y trataba a sus alumnos con mucho cariño. La quería mucho y lloré cuando tuve que cambiar de clase.

¿Qué actividades te gustaban más?

Cuando era muy pequeña me gustaba jugar con el agua y la arena. Era muy divertido y parecía que lo único que queríamos hacer era jugar. Después empecé a disfrutar de los ratos al final del día, cuando la profesora nos leía una historia.

¿Cuáles eran tus asignaturas más fuertes?

El inglés me resultaba fácil y me encantaba hacer ejercicios de comprensión. También me gustaba la música y aprendí a tocar el teclado.

72. School trips

1 (a) F   (c) D

  (b) C   (d) H

2 **Model answer:** El mes pasado hicimos una excursión a la ciudad para ir al cine y a un restaurante español.

Viajamos en autocar desde el instituto y una vez en la ciudad, fuimos a pie.

En el cine vimos una película española con una presentación y explicación de un profesor. Después fuimos a un restaurante español para tomar tapas y probar unos platos españoles típicos.

Me gustó mucho la visita. La película fue muy divertida y la comida estaba muy rica. Espero volver al restaurante con mi familia.

73. School events

1 (a) autumn

  (b) band competition

  (c) Christmas

  (d) rugby championship

  (e) seven months

2 *Sample answer / transcript*

¿Qué hay en la foto?

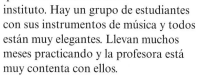

Listen to the recording

Es una orquesta de jóvenes que da un concierto en su instituto. Hay un grupo de estudiantes con sus instrumentos de música y todos están muy elegantes. Llevan muchos meses practicando y la profesora está muy contenta con ellos.

¿Qué actividades deportivas hay en tu instituto?

Tenemos partidos de fútbol y hockey todas las semanas y durante el verano hay campeonatos de tenis y de atletismo. A veces los profesores organizan torneos de baloncesto.

¿Qué evento te gustaría tener en tu instituto? … ¿Por qué?

Quisiera tener un concurso de talentos para los estudiantes donde podríamos participar como cantantes, bailarines o músicos. Sería muy divertido.

Describe un evento cultural en tu colegio.

Cada año organizan una exposición de todas las obras de arte de los estudiantes que hacen exámenes de dibujo. Los alumnos y profesores la visitan durante el día y por la tarde los padres pueden venir a verla.

¿Cuál es tu opinión sobre los días sin uniforme?

Me gustan mucho. Es muy divertido ir a clase en tu propia ropa. También es una manera fácil de recaudar dinero para las organizaciones benéficas.

74. School exchanges

1 (a) plane and coach / bus

  (b) 30 km from Barcelona

  (c) with a Spanish family

  (d) attend / take part in classes

  (e) trip to an ice rink

2 (a) B, D

  (b) C, D

  (c) B, E

75. Future plans

1 (a) B   (e) D

  (b) C   (f) A

  (c) D   (g) C

  (d) A

2 (a) una pequeña minoría

  (b) el setenta y ocho por ciento

  (c) ni uno de ellos

  (d) el dinero

  (e) una relación estable

76. Future education plans

1 (a) C   (d) C

  (b) B   (e) A

  (c) A   (f) B

2 B, H, E, C

77. Using languages

1 (a) H   (c) B

  (b) F   (d) G

2 Studying Spanish will open many doors at a professional level. There are many countries which have Spanish as their official language and therefore there are many jobs in which speaking the language may be an essential factor. Being able to speak Spanish will help you to enjoy literature and cinema. It is an increasingly global and influential language in the world of the arts.

78. Jobs

1 (a) C   (e) B

  (b) A   (f) D

  (c) B   (g) B

  (d) A

2 (a) Ahora: camarero; En el futuro: policía

  (b) En el pasado: dependiente; En el futuro: cartero

79. Opinions about jobs

1 (a) D   (d) A

  (b) F   (e) B

  (c) G   (f) E

2 Role play

Sample answer / transcript

Listen to the recording

Intro: Estás hablando con tu amiga sobre trabajos distintos.

Teacher: ¿Qué aspectos del trabajo son importantes para ti y por qué?

Student: Para mí, un trabajo tiene que ser variado y bastante bien pagado.

Teacher: ¿Qué tipo de trabajo no te gustaría hacer y por qué?

Student: No me gustaría trabajar en una oficina y hacer la misma cosa todos los días.

Teacher: A mí tampoco. ¿Qué piensas sobre trabajar en el extranjero?

Student: Me gustaría durante un tiempo, pero solo un año o dos.

Teacher: ¿Cuál sería tu trabajo ideal y por qué?

Student: Me encantaría ser ingeniera porque es un trabajo útil y creativo.

Teacher: Sí, es verdad.

Student: ¿Crees que el dinero es importante en un trabajo?

Teacher: Bastante, pero no es lo más importante.

80. Applying for jobs

1　(a) double his current salary / double what he earns now

(b) arriving late

(c) the way you dress; the way you shake hands / the way you give your hand

(d) He goes out to their car with them. / He accompanies them to their car.

(e) because a car tells you a lot about the owner

(f) Their car is full of rubbish.

2　Soy creativo/a, trabajador(a) y ambicioso/a y me llevo bien con otras personas / otra gente. Tengo experiencia como camarero/a en un restaurante y he trabajado de recepcionista en un hotel. Hablo español y un poco de francés y entiendo la importancia de las buenas relaciones con los clientes. El trabajo sería ideal para mí.

81. Careers and training

1　(a) IT technician

(b) He likes the idea of solving a company's IT problems and he wants to create solutions to improve their systems.

(c) A level / bachillerato in IT

(d) a (shorter) training course with qualifications accepted in the industry

(e) You don't get paid.

(f) Where is the best place to look for job adverts in the profession?

2　C, A, E, H

Grammar

82. Nouns and articles

1　(a) la (b) el (c) las (d) los (e) la (f) el (g) las (h) los (i) el (j) la

2　(a) las (b) un (c) el (d) los (e) una (f) un (g) el (h) El

3　(b) Mi padre es ~~un~~ dentista y mi madre es ~~una~~ enfermera.

(c) Hay muy pocos estudiantes en el instituto sin ~~un~~ móvil.

(d) Escribo con ~~un~~ lápiz en mi clase de matemáticas.

(e) En el futuro me gustaría ser ~~una~~ actriz.

(h) Se puede reservar dos habitaciones con ~~una~~ ducha.

83. Adjectives

1　(a) cómoda (b) traviesos (c) rojo (d) interesantes (e) español (f) simpáticas (g) preciosa (h) baratos

2　(a) lujoso (b) cómodos (c) bueno (d) impresionante (e) limpia (f) útiles

3　(a) En Inglaterra hay **poca** gente que habla muy bien griego.

(b) Lo mejor es que tiene un jardín **bonito**.

(c) Estamos **contentas** porque hace buen tiempo.

(d) En el futuro habrá una **gran** estatua aquí en la plaza.

(e) Nuestro apartamento está en el **primer** piso.

84. Possessives and pronouns

1

English	Spanish singular	Spanish plural
my	mi	**mis**
your	**tu**	tus
his / her / its	**su**	**sus**
our	**nuestro / nuestra**	nuestros / nuestras
your	**vuestro / vuestra**	**vuestros / vuestras**
their	su	sus

2　(a) Mi (b) Su (c) Sus (d) Mis (e) Su

3　(a) el mío (b) las suyas (c) el nuestro (d) el tuyo

4　(a) María tiene un gato que es negro y pequeño.

(b) Vivimos en un pueblo que está en el norte de Inglaterra.

(c) En la clase de literatura tengo que leer un libro que es muy aburrido.

85. Comparisons

1　(a) Mi madre es **más delgada que** mi padre.

(b) Mariela es **menos paciente que** Francisco.

(c) Este autobús es **más lento que** el tren.

(d) La fruta es **tan sana / saludable como** las verduras.

(e) Esta camisa es **tan cara como** aquella chaqueta.

2　(a) el mejor (b) los peores (c) la más pequeña (d) los más inteligentes (e) las menos aburridas

3　(a) Mi primo/a es más perezoso/a que tu tío.

(b) Su móvil es pequeñísimo.

(c) El examen de español es facilísimo.

(d) Las películas de terror son tan emocionantes como las películas de acción.

(e) ¡Mi instituto es el más feo!

(f) Las ciencias son menos aburridas que la geografía.

(g) Messi es el mejor.

86. Other adjectives

1

English	Masc sing	Fem sing	Masc plural	Fem plural
this / these	este	**esta**	**estos**	estas
that / those	**ese**	esa	**esos**	**esas**
that (over there) / those (over there)	**aquel**	**aquella**	aquellos	**aquellas**

2 (a) estas botas (b) esta camiseta (c) aquella chica
(d) esos plátanos (e) ese móvil (f) aquellas revistas
(g) este libro (h) esa película (i) aquel tren
(j) estos sombreros (k) esas fresas (l) aquellos chicos

3 (a) cada (b) misma (c) algunas (d) todos (e) otra

4 (a) Todos (b) Algunos (c) Todos (d) algunos (e) misma
(f) mismos

87. Pronouns

1

yo	I
tú	you singular
él	he
ella	**she**
nosotros	we (masc.)
nosotras	**we (fem.)**
vosotros	**you plural (masc.)**
vosotras	you plural (fem.)
ellos	**they (masc.)**
ellas	they (fem.)

2 (a) Las hemos perdido.
(b) La han perdido.
(c) Teresa lo come.
(d) Lo compro.
(e) No la bebo.
(f) No la lavo.
(g) Lo quiero escribir. / Quiero escribirlo.
(h) No quiero leerla. / No la quiero leer.
(i) La necesito ahora.
(j) Vamos a venderla. / La vamos a vender.

3 (a) I am going to write to him / her this afternoon.
(b) I visited them yesterday.
(c) I will do it if I have time.
(d) I gave him / her a present for his / her birthday.
(e) Have you seen them?
(f) Vino a visitarme en casa. / Me vino a visitar en casa.
(g) Me mandaron la reserva.
(h) Voy a comprarlos en línea. / Los voy a comprar en línea.

88. The present tense

1 (a) vivimos (b) bailan (c) vendo (d) lleváis (e) odias
(f) come (g) salimos (h) escucha

2 (a) comen (b) vivimos (c) tienes (d) hablan (e) debe
(f) grita (g) chateo (h) lee (i) piensa (j) Podéis

3 (a) cenamos (b) trabajan (c) desayuno (d) pone
(e) compramos (f) cuestan (g) Quiero (h) piden

89. Reflexive verbs (present)

1

me	afeito
te	afeitas
se	afeita
nos	afeitamos
os	afeitáis
se	afeitan
me	visto
te	vistes
se	viste
nos	vestimos
os	vestís
se	visten

2 (a) se (b) se (c) te (d) se (e) se
(f) Nos (g) Os (h) Te

3 Todos los días Olivia **se levanta** temprano para ir a trabajar. **Trabaja** en una tienda de ropa famosa. Primero **se lava** los dientes y luego **se ducha** y **se viste**. **Baja** las escaleras y **desayuna** cereales con fruta. Siempre **se peina** en la cocina. Después, **se lava** la cara en el cuarto de baño que está abajo, al lado de la cocina. **Se pone** la chaqueta y **sale** a las ocho y media porque el autobús llega a las nueve menos cuarto. **Vuelve** a casa a las siete de la tarde.

90. Irregular verbs (present)

1 (a) conduce, conduzco
(b) da, doy
(c) oye, sale
(d) hace, cojo
(e) venís, traéis

2 (a) oye
(b) conozco
(c) vienen
(d) cojo
(e) vamos
(f) sé
(g) tienes
(h) pongo
(i) traigo
(j) dicen

3 (a) Voy a España.
(b) Tiene dos hermanas.
(c) Oigo música.
(d) Dice mentiras.
(e) Cogemos el autobús.
(f) Hacen los deberes.
(g) Sales los sábados.
(h) Doy clases.
(i) Trae pan.
(j) Pongo la mesa.

91. *Ser and estar*

1 (a) está (b) son (c) Soy (d) es (e) Son (f) está (g) Estáis
(h) Estamos

2 (a) Where is the bank? ('estar' for location)
(b) My grandmothers are very generous. ('ser' for characteristics)
(c) I am from Madrid but I work in Barcelona. ('ser' for where you are from)
(d) The dress is green with white flowers. ('ser' for colours)

(e) It's four thirty in the afternoon. ('ser' for time)

(f) The wardrobe is opposite the door. ('estar' for location)

(g) You are (all) very sad today because the holidays have finished. ('estar' for moods)

(h) We are ready for the drama exam. ('estar' for meaning 'ready' not 'clever')

3 (a), (d), (e), (g) – ✓

(b) Mi amigo es inteligente y tiene el pelo negro.

(c) Me duele la cabeza y estoy enfermo.

(f) Mi madre es médica y mi padre es ingeniero.

(h) Mi casa es bastante pequeña – tiene solo un dormitorio.

92. The gerund

1 (a) comiendo – eating

(b) saltando – jumping

(c) corriendo – running

(d) tomando – taking (drinking/eating)

(e) durmiendo – sleeping

(f) asistiendo – attending

(g) escribiendo – writing

(h) escuchando – listening

(i) aprendiendo – learning

(j) pudiendo – being able to

2 (a) Está montando en bicicleta.

(b) Estoy escuchando música.

(c) Están navegando por Internet.

(d) Estamos viendo una película.

(e) Estás hablando con amigos.

3 (a) Estaba haciendo vela cuando llegó la tormenta.

(b) Estaban comiendo cuando su madre les llamó.

(c) Estábamos tomando el sol cuando empezó a llover.

(d) Estabas cantando cuando salió el tren.

(e) Estábamos viendo la tele cuando nuestro padre volvió a casa.

(f) Estaba jugando a los videojuegos cuando llamó.

(g) Estabais escuchando al profesor cuando entró el perro.

(h) Estaba nadando en el mar cuando el tiburón apareció.

93. The preterite tense

1 (a) sacaron (b) volvimos (c) compró (d) llegaste (e) trabajasteis (f) fue (g) di (h) tuvimos (i) visitaron (j) bebió

2 (a) fui (b) tuvimos (c) dieron (d) fue (e) dio, pagué (f) hicieron (g) dijo (h) fue (i) Hice (j) tuve

3 **Fui** al cine con mis amigos y **vimos** una película de acción. Después **comimos** en un restaurante italiano. **Comí** una pizza con jamón y queso, y mi amiga Lola **comió** pollo con pasta. **Bebimos** zumo de manzana y mi amigo Tom **comió** una tarta de chocolate pero yo no **comí** postre. Después del restaurante **fui** en tren a casa de mi prima. El viaje **fue** largo y aburrido. **Volví** a casa y **me acosté** a las once de la noche.

94. The imperfect tense

1 (b) De pequeños <u>nadábamos</u> en el mar todas las semanas. ✓

(c) <u>Había</u> mucha gente en el museo y las estatuas <u>eran</u> preciosas. ✓

(e) Cuando <u>eran</u> más jóvenes, no <u>comían</u> tomate ni lechuga.

(h) Me <u>ponía</u> nervioso cada vez que <u>hacía</u> una prueba de vocabulario. ✓

(j) <u>Nevaba</u> todos los días y <u>hacía</u> un frío horrible. ✓

2 (a) On Wednesday we went to the swimming pool and we swam for an hour and a half. (preterite for a completed action in the past)

(b) When we were kids, we used to swim in the sea every week. (imperfect for 'used to')

(c) There were lots of people in the museum and the statues were beautiful. (imperfect for descriptions)

(d) My father prepared a vegetarian supper for us. (preterite for a completed action in the past)

(e) When they were younger, they didn't eat tomatoes or lettuce. (imperfect to describe repeated actions in the past)

(f) Gabriela arrived in Madrid by train to start her new job. (preterite for a completed action in the past)

(g) Yesterday we met in the café and we talked all afternoon. (preterite for a completed action in the past)

(h) I used to get nervous every time I did a vocabulary test. (imperfect for 'used to')

(i) I had a great time because it was sunny and it didn't rain. (preterite for a completed action in the past)

(j) It snowed every day and it was terribly cold. (imperfect for descriptions)

3 (a) tenía (b) vivía (c) Hacía (d) pasé (e) trabajaban (f) gastó (g) comíamos (h) jugué

95. The future tense

1 (a) jugar (b) Va (c) a (d) voy (e) Vas (f) Vais (g) va (h) ir (i) vamos (j) Voy

2 (a) Vamos a ver la película.

(b) No trabajaré los lunes.

(c) Van a coger el metro.

(d) Irá a Inglaterra.

(e) Van a jugar con mi hermano.

(f) Irás a España.

3 (a) va a ir (b) voy a ir (c) voy a tomar (d) voy a tener (e) Voy a trabajar (f) Va a ser (g) va a ser (h) va a seguir (i) va a vivir

96. The conditional tense

1 (a) compraríamos – we would buy

(b) saldrían – they would go out

(c) trabajaríais – you (all) would work

(d) estaría – he / she / it would be

(e) jugarías – you would play

(f) vendríamos – we would come

(g) podrías – you could

(h) habría – there would be

2 (a) iría (b) tomarían (c) trabajaría (d) ganaríamos (e) habría (f) usaría (g) malgastarían (h) lucharían (i) ganaría (j) compartiríamos

3 NB All answers can use either podrías or deberías. Some answers are interchangeable.

(a) Podrías evitar el estrés.

(b) Podrías comer más fruta y verduras.

(c) Deberías hacer más ejercicio.

(d) Deberías ir al médico.

(e) Deberías acostarte temprano.

(f) Podrías ir al dentista.

(g) Deberías consumir menos energía.

(h) Podrías comprar ropa de segunda mano.

97. Perfect and pluperfect

1

	Perfect tense	Pluperfect tense	+ past participles
yo	he	**había**	
tú	**has**	**habías**	
él / ella / usted	**ha**	había	hablado
nosotros / nosotras	hemos	**habíamos**	comido
vosotros / vosotras	**habéis**	**habíais**	vivido
ellos / ellas / ustedes	**han**	habían	

2 (a) We have lost our car.
(b) Have you studied Spanish?
(c) They have bought a laptop.
(d) I have done my homework
(e) We have seen a very informative documentary.
(f) Me he roto el brazo.
(g) Han perdido la maleta.
(h) Hemos comido muchos caramelos.
(i) ¿Has visitado el museo hoy?
(j) Los azafatos han abierto las puertas.

3 (b) había perdido (c) había nadado (d) había ido
(e) había dejado (f) había encontrado

98. Giving instructions

1 (a) Dobla a la derecha.
(b) Cruza la plaza.
(c) Pasa el puente.
(d) Ten cuidado.
(e) Ven aquí.
(f) Canta más bajo.
(g) Lee en voz alta.
(h) Escucha bien.
(i) Pon la mesa.
(j) Haz este ejercicio.

2 (a) Doblad a la derecha.
(b) Cruzad la plaza.
(c) Pasad el puente.
(d) Tened cuidado.
(e) Venid aquí.
(f) Cantad más bajo.
(g) Leed en voz alta.
(h) Escuchad bien.
(i) Poned la mesa.
(j) Haced este ejercicio.

3 (a) ¡Descarga la música!
(b) ¡Doblad a la izquierda!
(c) ¡Quita la mesa!
(d) ¡Haz la cama!
(e) ¡Pasad la aspiradora!

99. The present subjunctive

1 (a) hable (b) coman (c) vaya (d) vivas (e) trabajéis
(f) salga (g) pueda (h) hagan (i) encuentre (j) seamos

2 (a) No comas este pastel.
(b) No compres aquel vestido.
(c) No tomes esa calle.
(d) No bebas un vaso de zumo de naranja.
(e) No veas esta película romántica.
(f) No firméis aquí.

(g) No rellenéis este formulario.
(h) No abráis las ventanas.

3 (a) trabajen (b) haga (c) tengamos (d) sean (e) vaya
(f) compren

100. Negatives

1 (a) No estudio geografía.
(b) No vamos a las afueras.
(c) Ricardo no compró una moto nueva.
(d) Sus padres no vieron la tele.
(e) No voy a ir a Francia la semana que viene.

2 1 E   2 D   3 B   4 G   5 A/F   6 A/F   7 C

3 (a) Mis profesores no enseñan nunca cómo repasar.
(b) En mi casa no tuvimos jamás una sala de juegos.
(c) No me he quemado nunca los brazos.
(d) Aquí no tengo ni vestidos, ni faldas, ni camisetas.
(e) No vas a comprar ningún coche.
(f) Mis padres no escuchan a nadie.

4 (a) Por la tarde nunca bebemos / tomamos café. / Por la tarde no bebemos / tomamos nunca café.
(b) No plancho, ni cocino, ni limpio.
(c) No hablan ningún idioma. / No hablan ningunos idiomas.
(d) No podemos hablar con nadie durante el examen.
(e) No fumaré jamás / nunca porque es una pérdida de dinero. / Jamás / Nunca fumaré porque es una pérdida de dinero.

101. Special verbs

1

me		I like
te	gusta (sing)	you like
le	gustan (plural)	he / she / it likes
nos		we like
os		you (all) like
les		they like

2 (a), (c) – ✓
(b) Nos **apetece** ir al teatro mañana.
(d) No nos **gusta** la contaminación atmosférica.
(e) ¿Te **hacen** falta unas toallas?

3 (a) Nos hace falta un abrigo.
(b) Os encantan los caballos negros.
(c) A María le gustan aquellos zapatos.
(d) Te quedan veinte euros para comprar el regalo.
(e) Me duele la cabeza todo el tiempo.
(f) Les encantan los rascacielos porque son modernos.

102. *Por and para*

1 (a) For my birthday I want a new mobile phone.
(b) My friend works for an architect.
(c) Apps for the iPhone are incredible.
(d) I eat a lot of vegetables and fish in order to keep fit.
(e) You need the key to get into the house.
(f) Smoking is very bad for your health.
(g) They are going to organise a party to celebrate the end of the school year.
(h) For me, sports are always fun.

2 (a) El coche rojo pasó por las calles antiguas.
(b) Normalmente por la mañana me gusta desayunar cereales y fruta.
(c) Mandé la reserva por correo electrónico.
(d) Me gustaría cambiar este jersey por otro.
(e) En la tienda ganamos diez euros por hora.
(f) Había mucha basura por todas partes.

3 (a) Para (b) para (c) por (d) por / para (e) para

103. Questions and exclamations

1. Why? – **¿Por qué?**
   What? – **¿Qué?**
   When? – **¿Cuándo?**
   How? – **¿Cómo?**
   Where? – **¿Dónde?**
   Where to? – **¿Adónde?**
   Which? – **¿Cuál?**
   Which ones? – **¿Cuáles?**
   How much? – **¿Cuánto?**
   How many? – **¿Cuántos?**

2.
1	F
2	E
3	G
4	J
5	A
6	C
7	I
8	B
9	H
10	D

3. (a) horror (b) Cuánto (c) Cómo (d) guay (e) rollo

104. Connectives and adverbs

1. (a) rápidamente (b) difícilmente (c) lentamente
   (d) alegremente (e) tranquilamente

2.
1	L
2	E
3	A
4	K
5	D
6	B
7	G
8	J
9	F
10	I
11	C
12	H

3. (a) Sus padres cantan mal en la iglesia.
   (b) No hablo mucho porque soy tímido.
   (c) El tren pasa rápidamente por el túnel.
   (d) Los pendientes son demasiado caros.
   (e) A menudo comemos huevos por la mañana. /
       Comemos a menudo huevos por la mañana.
   (f) si / porque
   (g) porque
   (h) pero

105. Numbers

1. (a) veinte 20 (b) cuarenta y ocho 48
   (c) nueve 9 (d) cien 100 (e) catorce 14
   (f) mil 1,000 (g) trescientos 300 (h) cincuenta y siete 57
   (i) veintitrés 23 (j) quince 15
   (k) diecinueve 19 (l) quinientos 500
   (m) un millón 1,000,000 (n) novecientos 900
   (o) ochenta y ocho 88 (p) setenta y seis 76 (q) sesenta
   y siete 67 (r) diez 10 (s) cero 0 (t) veintinueve 29

2. (a) mil novecientos noventa y nueve
   (b) el diez de octubre
   (c) el primero/uno de enero
   (d) el tres de marzo
   (e) dos mil trece
   (f) el dieciséis de noviembre
   (g) el treinta de mayo
   (h) mil novecientos sesenta y ocho
   (i) dos mil dos
   (j) el veintiuno de abril

3. (a) Son las siete y cuarto.
   (b) Es la una y veinticinco.
   (c) Son las nueve menos veinticinco.
   (d) Son las once y diez.
   (e) Son las cuatro menos cuarto.
   (f) Son las diez menos diez.
   (g) Son las cinco y media.
   (h) Son las doce.

Tests

106. Listening 1

1. (a) sandwich / baguette
   (b) spaghetti in tomato sauce
   (c) omelette

2. C, H, F

107. Listening 2

1. (a) E   (b) B   (c) D
2. (a) E   (b) I, D   (c) F, G

108. Listening 3

1. F, A, E

2. (a) B   (d) A
   (b) C   (e) C
   (c) B   (f) B

109. Speaking 1

1. *Sample answers / transcripts*

Listen to the recording

   Intro: Usted está hablando con la empleada de una oficina de turismo en Andalucía, España.

   Teacher: Hola, ¿en qué puedo ayudar?

   Student: Quisiera información sobre los sitios de interés en Andalucía.

   Teacher: Este folleto será muy útil.

   Student: También quisiera un mapa de la región.

   Teacher: Muy bien. Aquí tiene. ¿Cómo prefiere viajar?

   Student: Prefiero viajar en autobús.

   Teacher: De acuerdo. ¿Cuánto tiempo va a estar aquí?

   Student: Voy a estar aquí una semana.

   Teacher: ¡Qué bien! ¿Quiere algo más?

   Student: ¿Hay excursiones en barco?

   Teacher: Sí, aquí tiene una lista de viajes en barco.

2 Intro: Estás hablando con tu amigo español sobre tu tiempo libre.

Listen to the recording

Teacher: ¿Qué haces en casa en tu tiempo libre?

Student: Suelo tocar el piano y navegar por Internet.

Teacher: ¿Y qué haces cuando sales con tus amigos?

Student: Vamos de compras en el centro y a veces al cine.

Teacher: ¿Qué hiciste durante las últimas vacaciones?

Student: Fui a la piscina varias veces y jugué al tenis con mi hermano.

Teacher: ¿Qué pasatiempo te gustaría probar en el futuro?

Student: Me gustaría aprender a tocar la guitarra.

Teacher: Buena idea.

Student: ¿Tienes muchos deberes?

Teacher: Hago dos horas de deberes cada día.

110. Speaking 2

1 *Sample answer / transcript*

¿Qué hay en la foto?

Listen to the recording

Hay una biblioteca. Los chicos leen libros y llevan uniforme. La biblioteca es grande y tiene muchos libros.

¿Cuál es tu asignatura favorita y por qué?

Mi asignatura favorita es la historia porque las clases son muy variadas. En algunas clases hablamos y escuchamos, y en otras leemos y escribimos.

¿Qué hiciste en tu última clase de español?

Hicimos un ejercicio de comprensión sobre el medio ambiente y también tuvimos un test de vocabulario.

¿Cuáles son los mejores aspectos de tu instituto?

Es un instituto muy bueno y los estudiantes se comportan bien en general. Los profesores son muy buenos.

¿Cómo te preparas para los exámenes?

Hago un horario de repaso para todas mis asignaturas y estudio un poco cada día.

2 *Sample answer / transcript*

¿Qué hay en la foto?

Listen to the recording

La foto es de la biblioteca de un instituto y hay varios alumnos estudiando allí. Los chicos llevan el uniforme escolar y parecen muy ocupados con sus estudios. La biblioteca es grande y ordenada, con muchos libros en los estantes. No hay ordenadores, solo libros.

¿Cuáles son las presiones de los estudios?

Creo que hay muchos deberes hoy día y es muy difícil encontrar tiempo libre para hacer otras actividades. También hay muchas pruebas y muchos exámenes y es muy importante sacar buenas notas en todo.

¿Qué te gustaría cambiar de tu instituto y por qué?

Cambiaría el horario. Cuando visité un instituto en España, descubrí que empiezan a las ocho y terminan sobre las dos. Sería fantástico tener un horario así porque tendrías toda la tarde para hacer otras cosas.

¿Qué hiciste en tu última clase de español?

Hicimos un ejercicio de comprensión sobre el medio ambiente y después trabajamos en parejas para hablar de las cosas que reciclamos. También tuvimos un test de vocabulario.

¿Cómo te preparas para los exámenes?

Hago un horario de repaso para todas mis asignaturas y estudio un poco cada día. También miro exámenes de otros años y uso las páginas web de repaso en la red.

111. Reading 1

1 (a) C   (c) A

   (b) F   (d) D

2 If I want to buy clothes, I go to town / to the city on the train or the bus and my friends and I go to the shopping centre. Last Saturday I bought a present for my mother because it is her birthday tomorrow. I will go to the shop with my father to choose a cake.

112. Reading 2

1 (a) the last Sunday in August

   (b) Children play and parents relax.

   (c) married women who want to have a child

   (d) stay in the sea until nine waves have passed

   (e) They will have a child within the next year.

2 (a) C   (b) C   (c) B

113. Reading 3

1 (a) sitting on the floor at the front

   (b) standing at the back

   (c) between 6 and 14

   (d) by smiling

   (e) He looked over 14.

   (f) He shook his head and pointed to a younger girl.

2 Last Friday I went with my parents to a quiz organised by the church to raise funds for the victims of the earthquake. There were four people in every team and we had to answer questions on sport, geography, music and recent news. We didn't win, but it was a very entertaining evening and they raised more than a hundred and fifty euros.

114. Reading 4

1 (a) C   (c) E

   (b) B   (d) D

115. Reading 5

1 (a) B   (c) D

   (b) A   (d) E

116. Writing 1

1 Model answer

En la foto hay una familia.

Comen en el jardín porque hace buen tiempo.

Están muy contentos.

El padre sirve la ensalada.

2 Model answer: Quiero hacer una reserva para el sábado dos de julio, para siete noches en total. Vamos a llegar sobre las once de la mañana. Queremos una habitación doble y una habitación individual con vistas al mar. También queremos un balcón. No queremos cena, solo desayuno.

117. Writing 2

1   Me gusta el pescado.

La comida aquí es muy buena.

No voy a tomar helado, prefiero fruta.

Comí en un restaurante francés la semana pasada.

Nunca como carne porque soy vegetariano/a.

2   En mi instituto las clases de español son divertidas y variadas y aprendemos mucho sobre el idioma y el país. Es muy útil saber otro idioma porque te da más oportunidades de encontrar un trabajo bien pagado. Empecé con el español cuando tenía once años y en el futuro me gustaría aprender italiano también.

118. Writing 3

1   **Model answer:** Durante tu visita vamos a pasar un fin de semana en Edimburgo, en Escocia. Es una ciudad muy histórica y bonita con muchas atracciones. Vamos a viajar en tren porque hay un tren directo desde la estación de nuestro pueblo. Creo que el viaje es de una hora y media. En Edimburgo podemos visitar el castillo, ir de compras en la famosa calle central y comer en restaurante de mariscos. Tenemos buen tiempo aquí de momento y ayer hizo mucho sol todo el día.

119. Writing 4

1   **Model answer**

¡Hola Álvaro!

Aquí en mi país tenemos tres opciones principales a los dieciséis años. Primero, puedes dejar el instituto si quieres porque la educación no es obligatoria después de esa edad. Sin embargo, no hay muchos trabajos porque la mayoría de las empresas prefiere emplear a jóvenes un poco más mayores. Segundo, puedes buscar un aprendizaje donde trabajas y recibes un sueldo, pero uno o dos días por semana asistes a un curso de formación. Es una opción con posibilidades. La tercera opción es continuar con los estudios en el instituto. Esto es lo que yo voy a hacer porque siempre he querido ser farmacéutico y necesito un título universitario. El mes pasado tuve la suerte de ayudar en una farmacia en mi pueblo y lo encontré fascinante porque es un trabajo de mucha responsabilidad. Tienes que entender los efectos de las drogas y las medicinas porque la gente a menudo pide consejos al farmacéutico.

Notes

Notes

Notes

Notes

Published by Pearson Education Limited, 80 Strand, London, WC2R 0RL.

www.pearsonschoolsandfecolleges.co.uk

Text and illustrations © Pearson Education Limited 2017
Typeset and illustrated by Kamae Design, Oxford
Produced by Out of House Publishing
Cover illustration by Miriam Sturdee

The right of Vivien Halksworth to be identified as author of this work has been asserted by her in accordance with the Copyright, Designs and Patents Act 1988.

First published 2017

20 19 18
10 9 8 7 6 5 4 3

British Library Cataloguing in Publication Data
A catalogue record for this book is available from the British Library

ISBN 9781292131412

Printed in Slovakia by Neografia.

Acknowledgements
Content written by Jacqui Lopez and Leanda Reeves is included.

The publisher would like to thank the following for their kind permission to reproduce their photographs:

123RF: Frenk Kaufmann 004, Wavebreak Media Ltd 005, Jozef Polc 048; **Alamy Stock Photo:** Richard Wayman 026, Cultura Creative (RF) 038, Garo/Phanie 042, Hill Street Studios/Blend Images 073, Gregg Vignal 110, Image Source 116; **Getty Images:** Leah Warkentin 039, **Rex Features:** John Birdsall 044; **Shutterstock:** Suhendri 002, Goodluz 007, Anutr Yossundara 011, Spectral Design 020, Monkey Business Images 022, KikoStock 031, Maksim Shmeljov 063, Monkey Business Images 071

All other images © Pearson Education

Note from the publisher
Pearson has robust editorial processes, including answer and fact checks, to ensure the accuracy of the content in this publication, and every effort is made to ensure this publication is free of errors. We are, however, only human, and occasionally errors do occur. Pearson is not liable for any misunderstandings that arise as a result of errors in this publication, but it is our priority to ensure that the content is accurate. If you spot an error, please do contact us at resourcescorrections@pearson.com so we can make sure it is corrected.